A Deep Dependence

A Deep Dependence

90 *Our Daily Bread* Reflections
on Loving and Trusting God

Bill Crowder

Our Daily Bread
Publishing™

A Deep Dependence: 90 Our Daily Bread *Reflections on Loving and Trusting God*
©2020 by Our Daily Bread Ministries

Cover design: Michelle Lenger
Interior design: Jessica Ess, Hillspring Books

Library of Congress Cataloging-in-Publication Data Available

ISBN: 978-1-64070-054-3

Printed in the United States of America

21 22 23 24 25 26 27 / 8 7 6 5 4 3 2

FOREWORD

◆   ◆   ◆

Anyone familiar with Our Daily Bread Ministries over the last couple of decades has noticed and appreciated Bill Crowder's contributions to the devotionals, Bible study materials, *Discover the Word* radio program, as well as the books he's written for Our Daily Bread Publishing (formerly Discovery House). Yet what many of our friends have not seen is how tirelessly Bill has worked behind the scenes while endearing himself as a team member, resource, and encouragement to coworkers and countless friends.

I say this about a dear friend I've had a chance to work with over the same twenty-five or so years. In the process I've been increasingly pleased to see the appreciation and the affirmation Bill has received not only in the United States but also among Our Daily Bread Ministries' international coworkers and friends around the world.

Some of my appreciation is colored by the fun Bill and I have had cheering and comforting one another on the golf course or in a neighborhood coffee shop where we've compared books we've read, tested one another's thinking, and shared our mutual desire for a life that would be far better than either of us has been able to actually live.

While facing the realities of my own age and limitations, I've been increasingly grateful for Bill's giftedness in opening Scripture to show our need of Christ—to know the heart of our God. I love his inclination to dress down in jeans or a sports jersey, often reflecting his love of Los Angeles Angels baseball or Liverpool football. I've listened for hours as Bill has entertained me and other coworkers out of his supersized interest in and recall of music, film, history, and sports.

Over the years I've also heard Bill talk about what he calls The Crowder Curse (anything bad that can happen will), while seeing that he has been entrusted by our Father with unusual capacity for a ridiculous amount of trivial information that makes its way into some of the most important insights and connections in devotionals, books, teaching sessions, and Bible conferences.

All of this has contributed richly to me personally since receiving a telephone call from Bill thirty or so years ago while he was pastoring a church in West Virginia. After accepting the invitation to speak to his church family, we stayed in touch as he, Marlene, and their five children eventually moved to serve congregations in Southern California and in Holland, Michigan. Once he had located in West Michigan, Bill and I began spending lunches together. He agreed to try writing for our Discovery Series Bible studies, and then at a time of mutual need, he agreed to join our staff.

Before accepting the invitation to write this foreword, I hesitated. I was afraid of boring you with details, because I saw myself as too close to Bill to be objective. But even if I have lost myself in the friendship, I hope I've had a chance to give you some sense of how Bill Crowder came to be such an important part of *Our Daily Bread* and a personal friend and coworker not only to me but also to our fellow employees in Grand Rapids and in our thirty-five international offices.

Most importantly, I value the chance to let you know that I've seen how seriously and with what humility Bill takes his opportunity to explore with all of us the wonder of Scriptures that—in inexhaustible, life-changing, and yet ever surprising ways—connects with our deepest emotions and thoughts to point us to the Living Word and Son of God. ◆

Mart DeHaan
Senior Advisor for Ministry Content
Our Daily Bread Ministries

The Process

One of the great and humbling privileges of my recent years of ministry has been writing for *Our Daily Bread*. My journey into writing began in the mid-90s when Mart DeHaan, then-president of then-RBC Ministries, asked if I would be interested in writing Bible study booklets for the ministry's Discovery Series booklet curriculum. I told him I didn't know if I even knew how—all I had ever written were thesis papers in seminary (that nobody is expected to read) or sermons for the churches I had pastored (a totally different animal). But at Mart's encouraging prodding, we started on an adventure that would eventually take me from pastoral work to the Our Daily Bread Ministries teaching staff, more booklets, books with Discovery House, and eventually to writing devotionals for *Our Daily Bread*.

It is more than a little overwhelming to be allowed to put thoughts on paper—especially when you know people will read them. The responsibility is weighty, and the joy is heartening. And now, after more than a dozen years of writing for *Our Daily Bread*, I have friends and prayer partners around the world—people I would have never known or been able to speak to without this rare opportunity to write.

For me, the writing process is one of trying to live life with my eyes open and my heart responsive to what the Lord brings my way. Through the things I read, the music I hear, the sports I enjoy, and the places I visit, the entire world becomes a treasure trove of real-life moments that connect our hearts and minds to the Scriptures. It seems to be an ever-replenishing supply, and that is, in my opinion, what makes *Our Daily Bread* so effective: It connects real life in the real world to the real wisdom and heart of a real heavenly Father. I see or hear or read something, and it is as if the scriptural point is self-evident. Our God is amazing that way!

So, as I read about the lost colony of Roanoke (an island off the coast of North Carolina)—115 men, women, and children who had come to the New World in 1587 to start a life and disappeared from the face of the earth—I was stunned by the depth of one of America's greatest and most frustrating mysteries. And my heart was turned to Paul's marvelous words: "Great is the mystery of godliness: He who was revealed in the flesh . . ." (1 Timothy 3:16 NASB). While the mysteries of life can cause us disappointment and frustration, the mystery of the Christ can instead fill us with awe and wonder. God's Son came in flesh to rescue us! That kind of love is the best kind of mystery.

And that became an article for *Our Daily Bread,* so I could share the mystery and wonder with you all. As I write this intro, that article is experiencing the nitty gritty of the vitally important editorial process to make it as readable and helpful as possible for all of you—and countless others around the world.

As I said, it is a humbling privilege—and I am grateful for any help our good, good Father might give to someone through this fascinating way of expressing the Scriptures.

My heart's desire would be that, in the pages of this collection of articles, you might find encouragement, direction, challenge, and wisdom for life. But most of all, I trust that you will encounter our wonderful, loving, mysterious God. He is the One who gives life meaning. ◆

—*Bill Crowder*

◆ REFLECTIONS ◆

A Deep Dependence

2 Corinthians 3:1–8

Not that we are competent in ourselves to claim anything for ourselves, but our competence comes from God. 2 Corinthians 3:5

Five for Fighting is the stage name of a recording artist who soared to popularity after the terrorist attacks of September 11, 2001. He sings the song "Superman (It's Not Easy)," a ballad that imagines what it must be like to be a superhero. Yet he struggles with the inadequacy of his strength to cope with the world's complexities.

People seemed to identify with the song's theme. Real life proves we are insufficient to battle the overwhelming burdens that confront us. Even those who want to be self-sufficient can't manage life in their own strength.

As followers of Christ, we have a resource that even Superman could never claim. In our relationship with God, we find a sufficiency for life that can overwhelm our inadequacies and enable us to live victoriously. This was Paul's encouragement to our hearts when he wrote to the believers at Corinth. He said, "Not that we are competent in ourselves to claim anything for ourselves, but our competence comes from God" (2 Corinthians 3:5). That makes all the difference in the world.

Left to ourselves, we are forced to live with the reality that we can never be adequate to grapple with life. But with a deep dependence on God's strength, we find all we need to navigate the storms of life in this turbulent world.

◆　◆　◆

We must experience our weakness to experience God's strength.

Dependence Day

John 15:1–8

I am the vine, you are the branches. If you remain
in me and I in you, you will bear much fruit;
apart from me you can do nothing. *John 15:5*

In the US, the Fourth of July is a national holiday when outdoor grills are heated up; beaches are packed; and cities and towns have parades and fireworks displays, picnics, and patriotic celebrations. All of this is in remembrance of July 4, 1776, when the thirteen American colonies declared their independence.

Independence appeals to all ages. It means "freedom from the control, influence, support, and aid of others." So, it's not surprising that teenagers talk about gaining their independence. Many adults have the goal of being "independently wealthy." And senior citizens want to maintain their independence. Whether anyone is ever truly independent is a discussion for another time and place—but it sounds good.

Craving political or personal independence is one thing; daring to pursue spiritual independence is problematic. What we need instead is a recognition and acceptance of our deep spiritual dependence. Jesus said, "I am the vine, you are the branches. If you remain in me and I in you, you will bear much fruit; apart from me you can do nothing" (John 15:5).

Far from being self-reliant, we are totally and eternally dependent on the One who died to set us free. Every day is our "dependence day."

◆　◆　◆

Our greatest strength comes from dependence on our strong God.

The Source of Impact

Acts 4:1–13

When they saw the courage of Peter and John . . .
they were astonished and they took note that these
men had been with Jesus. *Acts 4:13*

Nobel Prizes are awarded annually to people who have made an extraordinary impact in a variety of fields. Leaders in economics, physics, literature, medicine, and peace are recognized for their contributions. When a person is deemed worthy to receive a Nobel Prize, it is the ultimate affirmation of years of training, effort, education, and sacrifice in pursuit of excellence—investments that are the source of their impact.

We might wish to make a significant impact spiritually in our world, but we wonder, What is the source of spiritual and ministry influence? If we want to make an extraordinary impact for Jesus Christ, what must we invest in?

Christ's first followers were affected by spending time with Jesus. Israel's religious leaders recognized this. Acts 4:13 tells us, "When [the leaders] saw the courage of Peter and John and realized that they were unschooled, ordinary men, they were astonished and they took note that these men had been with Jesus."

Training and education are valuable in the service of the Savior, but nothing can replace time spent in His presence. He is the source of whatever spiritual impact we might have on our world. How much time have you been spending with Jesus—your source of impact?

◆ ◆ ◆

To master this life, spend time with the Master.

Red Tape

Through [Jesus] we have gained access
by faith into this grace in which we now stand.
And we boast in the hope of the glory of God. *Romans 5:2*

The expression "red tape" describes the annoying way bureaucracy prevents things from getting done. Originally, the phrase referred to the common practice of binding official documents with red ribbon. In the early 1800s, the term was popularized by the writings of Scottish historian Thomas Carlyle, who was protesting governmental foot-dragging. Following the American Civil War, the problem of "red tape" resurfaced as war veterans struggled to receive their benefits. The term denotes frustration and disappointment because burdensome hurdles can stop us from accomplishing our goals.

Bureaucratic red tape is almost legendary, but there is one place in the universe where it's never an issue—the throne of God. In Romans 5:2, Paul speaks of Christ, "through whom we have gained access by faith into this grace in which we now stand." When our hearts are broken or our lives are troubled, there is no red tape hindering our access to God. Jesus Christ has paved the way so we can have access to enter boldly into the presence of the King of heaven (Hebrews 4:16).

Remember, when your heart is hurting, you don't have to cut through a lot of red tape to present your needs to God. Through Christ, we have full and immediate access.

◆ ◆ ◆

God's throne is always accessible to His children.

Heart Attitude

Ephesians 6:5–9

Obey them not only to win their favor
when their eye is on you, but as slaves of Christ,
doing the will of God from your heart. *Ephesians 6:6*

I love watching the skill and passion of great athletes as they give their all on the field or court. It shows their love for the game. Conversely, when a long season is winding down and a team is already eliminated from any opportunity for championship or playoff games, sometimes it seems that the players are merely "going through the motions." Their lack of passion can be disappointing to fans who have paid to watch a good game.

Passion is a key aspect of our personal lives as well. Our heart attitude toward the Lord is revealed in how we serve Him. The apostle Paul said that our service includes the way we go about our daily work. In Ephesians 6:6, we read that we are to approach our work, "not only to win their favor when [others' eyes are] on you, but as slaves of Christ, doing the will of God from your heart."

For me, the key in that verse is "from your heart." I have a heavenly Father who loves me deeply and sacrificed His Son for me. How can I do anything less than give my very best for Him? The passion to live for God that comes "from [our] heart" provides our best response to the One who has done so much for us.

◆　◆　◆

The love of God motivates us to live for God.

Clean Hands

Psalm 24

> Who may ascend the mountain of the LORD?
> Who may stand in his holy place?
> The one who has clean hands and a pure heart. *Psalm 24:3–4*

It seems that wherever you go these days, you see signs encouraging people to wash their hands. With the constant threat of germs and viruses spreading disease throughout the general public, health officials continually remind us that unwashed hands form the single greatest agent for the spread of germs. So, in addition to the signs calling for vigilant handwashing, public places will often provide hand sanitizers to help take care of germs and bacteria.

David also spoke of the importance of "clean hands," but for a dramatically different reason. He said that clean hands are one key to being able to enter into God's presence for worship: "Who may ascend the mountain of the LORD? Who may stand in his holy place?" he asked. And the answer? "The one who has clean hands and a pure heart" (Psalm 24:3–4). Here "clean hands" is not a reference to personal hygiene but a metaphor for our spiritual condition—being cleansed from sin (1 John 1:9). It speaks of a life committed to what is right and godly—enabling us to stand blameless before our Lord in the privilege of worship.

As His life is lived out in our lives, He can help us to do what's right so that our hands are clean and our hearts are ready to give worship to our great God.

◆　◆　◆

The road to worship begins with gratefulness
for the cleansing of God.

Always There

Psalm 55:16–23

Evening, morning and noon
I cry out in distress,
and he hears my voice. *Psalm 55:17*

Several years ago, the radio engineers who work at Our Daily Bread Ministries were getting ready to broadcast a program via satellite. They had prepared everything, including the satellite link. But just as they were to begin uploading, the signal to the satellite was lost. Confused, the engineers labored to reconnect the link, but nothing worked. Then they got the word—the satellite was gone. Literally. The satellite had suddenly and surprisingly fallen from the sky. It was no longer there.

I suspect that sometimes when we pray, we think something similar has happened to God—that for some reason He isn't there. But the Bible offers us comfort with the assurance that God hasn't "fallen from the sky." He is always available to us. He hears and He cares.

In a time of desperation, David wrote, "Evening, morning and noon I cry out in distress, and he hears my voice" (Psalm 55:17). No matter when we call on God, He hears the cries of His children. That should encourage our hearts. What was David's response to having a God who hears prayer? "Cast your cares on the LORD and he will sustain you" (v. 22). Although God may not answer as we would like or when we would like, we know that at "evening, morning and noon" He is always there.

◆　◆　◆

God is always available to hear the prayer of His child.

Opened Ears

Psalm 40:1–10

> Sacrifice and offering you did not desire—
> but my ears you have opened—
> burnt offerings and sin offerings you did not require. *Psalm 40:6*

Recently I was having trouble with my ears and decided to try a somewhat controversial treatment. It was supposed to melt the wax in my ears and clear out any impediments that might get in the way of the ability to hear. I have to admit that it sounded like a strange experience. But I was desperate to be able to hear clearly, so I was willing to give it a try.

As important as good hearing is in life, it is even more important in our walk with God. In Psalm 40:6, David declared, "Sacrifice and offering you did not desire—but my ears you have opened—burnt offerings and sin offerings you did not require." The word *opened* in this verse can be translated "cleared out," and it speaks of what God desires for us. He wants our ears to be open and ready to hear Him as He speaks to us through His Word. Sometimes, however, our spiritual ears may be blocked by the background noise of the surrounding culture or the siren songs of temptation and sin.

May we instead turn our hearts to the Lord in full devotion, keeping our ears open to Him so we will be sensitive to His voice. As He speaks, He will put His Word in our hearts, and we will learn from Him to delight in His will (v. 8).

♦ ♦ ♦

God speaks through His Word to those who listen with their heart.

Never Too Busy

Psalm 145:8–21

The LORD is near to all who call on him,
to all who call on him in truth. *Psalm 145:18*

College students rent a house from my sister and her husband. One night, a thief attempted to break in. When the young woman living there called the police to tell them that a break-in was in progress, the operator responded in an unusual way: "You'll have to call back in the morning. We're just too busy right now." That response was very disturbing! The young woman had done the right thing by calling the police, but for some reason her plea for help was disregarded. That kind of indifference is upsetting.

But indifference never happens when we go to God in prayer. We may not always feel that God is listening, but He is. He cares, and He will respond. The Bible reminds us that we can take comfort in the fact that our God is deeply concerned with what concerns our hearts: "The LORD is near to all who call on him, to all who call on him in truth" (Psalm 145:18). When we call out to Him, we will never get a disinterested response.

Rather than distancing himself from us when we cry to Him, our heavenly Father draws close to us in our time of need. He is never too busy for His child's prayers—He hears us when we call.

◆　◆　◆

You'll never get a busy signal on the prayer line to heaven.

A "Banana Slug" Lesson

Micah 6:1–8

> What does the LORD require of you?
> To act justly and to love mercy
> and to walk humbly with your God. *Micah 6:8*

Sports team names have a variety of origins. They come from history (Spartans, Mountaineers), nature (Cardinals, Terrapins), and even colors (Orange, Reds).

One even comes from the mollusk family.

In the 1980s, the University of California at Santa Cruz was just starting to get involved in competitive sports. UCSC had a bit of disdain for the overemphasis some big-time schools place on athletics, so the student body sought a team name that would reflect a somewhat different approach. They decided on the Banana Slug, a yellow, slimy, slow, shell-less mollusk. It was a clever way for UCSC to give a balanced perspective on the relative worth of sports.

I have always loved sports, but I know that they can easily become more important than they should be. What matters most in life is what Jesus said is most vital—loving God with all of our hearts and loving our neighbors as ourselves (Matthew 22:37–39). Micah listed God's requirements this way: "act justly," "love mercy," and "walk humbly with your God" (6:8). For believers in Jesus, it is vital that nothing else takes top priority over God's expectations for us.

What matters most to you? The Wolverines? The Red Sox? Or loving God in thought, word, and action?

◆　◆　◆

Beware of spending too much time on matters
of too little importance.

The Galatia Church

Galatians 3:1–12

Are you so foolish? After beginning by means of the Spirit, are you now trying to finish by means of the flesh? Galatians 3:3

I was driving through the countryside when I spotted a church building whose name surprised me. It said, "The Galatia Church." The name caught my attention because I was certain no one would choose to name a church this unless it was a geographic necessity.

A study of the biblical book of Galatians reveals that it is Paul's most fiery letter—criticizing the people for legalism, self-effort, and the exchange of grace for a different gospel. Galatia was not exactly the kind of church that you would see as an example to be followed.

This is true because the Galatians were trying to please God through their own efforts rather than by reliance on Him. Paul's charge against them was this: "Are you so foolish? After beginning by means of the Spirit, are you now trying to finish by means of the flesh?" (3:3).

Just as we cannot earn a relationship with God by our works, neither can we develop spiritually through our own strength. Paul's reminder to the Galatians (and us) is this: Dependence on God through the work of the Spirit in our lives is at the core of our walk with Christ.

If we think we can become like Jesus by our own efforts, we are, like the Galatians, fooling ourselves.

◆ ◆ ◆

The Holy Spirit is the Christian's power supply.

Morning

Lamentations 3:19–32

> [The LORD'S] compassions never fail.
> They are new every morning;
> great is your faithfulness. *Lamentations 3:22–23*

On a teaching trip to the Bible lands, our study group had just spent a restful night at our Tiberias hotel. When I awoke, I went to my window and gazed at the beauty of the sunrise on the Sea of Galilee. As I thought ahead to the places we would be visiting that day—the same places where Jesus had walked 2,000 years before—I was excited about the opportunities of the day that had begun with the splendor of the sunrise.

We don't need to be in Israel, however, to be amazed at what God gives us each day. Every morning of life offers us new challenges and rich blessings as we walk with Christ. Despite mistakes we may have made yesterday, choices we regret, and heartache we have endured, God is merciful to us. The sunrise reminds us of His faithfulness and of the new start each day brings.

Perhaps it was the simple joy of a beautiful sunrise that prompted Jeremiah to write, "Because of the LORD's great love we are not consumed, for his compassions never fail. They are new every morning; great is your faithfulness" (Lamentations 3:22–23).

Each new day the Lord gives to us—whether in the Bible lands or at home—is an expression of His faithfulness and provides opportunities to live for Him.

◆　◆　◆

The best reason for hope is God's faithfulness.

Noon

Psalm 62:1–8

Truly my soul finds rest in God;
my salvation comes from him. *Psalm 62:1*

Our office is a busy place where things sometimes feel like they are moving at breakneck speed. This often involves meeting after meeting, hallway conferences, and an avalanche of email.

In the midst of this extreme busyness, I sometimes feel the need to escape, to decompress. My response? To create a quiet place. On those days when I have no lunch meeting, I retreat to the quiet of my car. I grab some lunch and sit in my car, where I can read, listen to music, think, pray—and be refreshed.

I think this is the essence of what the shepherd-psalmist points to in Psalm 23:2. He sees the Good Shepherd bringing him to "quiet waters"—that is, waters to rest by. It pictures a quiet place, a retreat from the pressures of life, where you can rest in the presence of the Shepherd of your heart and be strengthened for what lies ahead. Even Jesus withdrew to a solitary place to pray and commune with His Father (Mark 1:35).

We all need retreats in our lives, not only because of the overwhelming nature of life but also because of our dependence on the resources of the Master. In our fast-paced days, it is essential to find a place of solitude—as the old hymn says, "a place of quiet rest, near to the heart of God." Where's yours?

◆　◆　◆

When we draw near to God, our minds are refreshed
and our strength is renewed!

Evening

Ephesians 5:6–17

After [Jesus] had dismissed [the crowd],
he went up on mountainside by himself to pray.
Later that night, he was there alone. *Matthew 14:23*

The evening is one of my favorite times of day. It's a time to look back, take stock, and reflect on the events of the day—whether good or bad. When weather permits, my wife and I walk, or sometimes we'll just fix a pot of coffee and talk with each other about our day and what we've accomplished. It's a time for careful thought and evaluation, for thanksgiving, and for prayer.

Our Lord had a similar practice during His earthly ministry. At the end of a wearying and demanding day, He went up on a mountain by himself for a few moments of reflection and prayer in the presence of His Father (Matthew 14:23).

The value of the quiet presence of our heavenly Father and the careful examination of how we have engaged life on a given day has great significance. Perhaps this was the goal of the apostle Paul's challenge for us to redeem the time (Ephesians 5:16); that is, to be sure we are making the best use of the time God gives us for living and serving.

As the day winds to a close, take some time for quiet reflection. In the serenity of the evening, we can, in God's presence, get a more accurate perspective on life and how we are living it.

◆ ◆ ◆

There will be more reflection of Jesus
when there is more reflection on Him.

Night

Psalm 42

By day the LORD directs his love,
at night his song is with me—
a prayer to the God of my life. *Psalm 42:8*

In his riveting and unsettling book *Night*, Elie Wiesel describes his boyhood experiences as one of the countless victims of the Holocaust. Ripped from his home and separated from everyone in his family except his father (who would die in the death camps), Wiesel suffered a dark night of the soul such as few will experience. It challenged his views and beliefs about God. His innocence and faith became sacrifices on the altar of man's evil and sin's darkness.

David experienced his own dark night of the soul, which many scholars believe motivated his writing of Psalm 42. Harried and hounded, probably as he was pursued by his rebellious son Absalom (2 Samuel 16–18), David echoed the pain and fear that can be felt in the isolation of night. It's the place where darkness grips us and forces us to consider the anguish of our heart and ask hard questions of God. The psalmist lamented God's seeming absence, yet in it all he found a night song (v. 8) that gave him peace and confidence for the difficulties ahead.

When we struggle in the night, we can be confident that God is at work in the darkness. We can say with the psalmist, "Put your hope in God, for I will yet praise him, my Savior and my God" (v. 11).

◆ ◆ ◆

When it is dark enough, men see the stars. —*Emerson*

Quiet, Please

1 Kings 19:1–18

After the earthquake came a fire, but the LORD was not in the fire.
And after the fire came a gentle whisper. 1 Kings 19:12

In recent years, the spread of personal digital music players has resulted in concerns about hearing loss. The design of the music players and their earphones has been the target of complaints and lawsuits. Long-term exposure to music at a high volume has been shown to cause serious hearing impairment. In a sense, too much hearing can result in an inability to hear.

We live in a world filled with noise—noises designed to sell, plead, seduce, and deceive. In the midst of this cacophony of sound, it's easy to miss the one voice that matters most.

Elijah had listened to Jezebel's threats and the voice of his own fear, so he fled to a cave to hide. In the cave he was confronted with the overwhelming noise of wind, an earthquake, and fire (1 Kings 19:11–12). Then the cave grew silent and the voice of the Lord— the only sound that mattered—broke through as "a gentle whisper" (v. 12).

If we are to hear God speaking to our hearts through His Word, we need to pull away from the noise of the crowd. Only when we learn to be quiet can we really understand what it means to commune with the God who cares for us.

In our "quiet time" today, let's make an effort to listen for the voice of God.

◆　◆　◆

To hear God's voice, turn down the world's volume.

Talent Search

Isaiah 6:1–8

I heard the voice of the Lord saying: "Whom shall I send?
And who will go for us?" *Isaiah 6:8*

Television shows like *American Idol* have become a global phenomenon. Millions wait anxiously to find out who will be the next singer eliminated in the musical talent hunt.

Some call it "a new concept in entertainment," but it's hardly a new idea. As a boy, I remember watching Ted Mack's *The Original Amateur Hour*. That show was followed by the bizarre talent hunt *The Gong Show* in the 70s, and then by *Star Search* in the 80s. It is an ongoing theme of television to search for someone unknown and make him or her famous.

Dreams of fame and fortune, however, are not at the heart of the search that is truly timeless. That search is God's own pursuit of hearts that are available for His work in the world.

In Isaiah, the Lord asks: "Whom shall I send? And who will go for us?" And then we read Isaiah's ready response: "Here am I. Send me!" (6:8).

God is not seeking the most qualified or talented; rather, He is seeking hearts that are surrendered to Him. He is seeking those who are available, dependable, and willing to be used. In those lives, God will show himself strong, and He will be glorified.

Are you available?

❖　❖　❖

Your life is God's gift to you—make it your gift to God.

A Fire to Be Kindled

Luke 24:13–32

They asked each other, "Were not our hearts
burning within us while he talked with us on the road
and opened the Scriptures to us?" *Luke 24:32*

In Acts 17, Paul went to Mars Hill to declare the truth of the resurrection. Many listeners gathered there were not spiritual seekers. Luke, who wrote the book of Acts, records that they spent their days simply wanting to discuss the latest new ideas, with little interest in acting on what they learned (v. 21).

Too much information can be dangerous. All the ideas can blur together and become incoherent, leaving us unchanged by what we know.

Centuries ago, the historian Plutarch warned of the danger of living on a purely informational level. He wisely said, "The mind is not a vessel to be filled but a fire to be kindled."

The Christ-followers on the road to Emmaus would have agreed (Luke 24). As they grieved the death of Jesus, the risen Christ himself joined them but hid His identity. He began instructing them about ancient Old Testament prophecies of recent events relating to Jesus. Later that day, Christ revealed himself to them and then departed.

After Jesus's departure, they marveled at what they had heard. The things He taught were not sterile facts but a fire that kindled their hearts with devotion for Him. May we likewise trust the Shepherd of our souls to kindle our hearts as we grow in His Word.

◆　◆　◆

You cannot start a fire in another's heart
till it is burning in your own.

Money Talks

Luke 12:13–21

The love of money is a root of all kinds of evil.
Some people, eager for money, have wandered from the faith
and pierced themselves with many griefs. *1 Timothy 6:10*

As I was driving home from the office, I saw a minivan proudly displaying a bumper sticker that read "Money Talks: Mine Says Goodbye." I think a lot of people can relate to that sentiment.

Much of our living is spent acquiring and using money, which doesn't last. The stock market crashes. Prices go up. Thieves steal others' goods. Things wear out and break down, requiring the acquisition and expenditure of more money to replace what has been lost. The temporary nature of material wealth makes it a poor bargain in the search for security in an insecure world. Money is much better at saying goodbye than it is at sticking around.

Nowhere does the Bible say it's wrong to have money or the things that money can buy. Where we lose our way is when money becomes the driving purpose of our lives. Like the rich man and his barns (Luke 12:13–21), we end up pursuing the accumulation of things that eventually will be forfeited—if not in life, then certainly at death.

How tragic to live our entire lives—only to end them with nothing of eternal worth to show for our labors. To paraphrase Jesus's words, it is much better to be rich toward God than to work for treasure that can't last (v. 21).

◆　◆　◆

Treasures in heaven are laid up
as treasures on earth are laid down.

When Life Is Too Big

1 Kings 3:4–14

Now, LORD my God, you have made your servant king
in place of my father David. But I am only a little child
and do not know how to carry out my duties. *1 Kings 3:7*

As a young man, Jimmy Carter was a junior officer in the US Navy. He was deeply impacted by Admiral Hyman Rickover, the mastermind of the US nuclear submarine fleet.

Shortly after Carter's inauguration as thirty-ninth President of the United States, he invited Rickover to the White House for lunch, where the admiral presented Carter with a plaque that read, "O God, Thy sea is so great, and my boat is so small." That prayer is a useful perspective on the size and complexity of life and our inability to manage it on our own.

Solomon too knew that life could be overwhelming. When he succeeded his father, David, as king of Israel, he confessed his weakness to God, saying, "Now, LORD my God, you have made your servant king in place of my father David. But I am only a little child and do not know how to carry out my duties." (1 Kings 3:7). As a result, he asked for the wisdom to lead in a way that would please God and help others (v. 9).

Is life feeling too big for you? There may not be easy answers to the challenges you are facing, but God promises that if you ask for wisdom He will grant it (James 1:5). You don't have to face the overwhelming challenges of life alone.

◆ ◆ ◆

Recognizing our own smallness
can cause us to embrace God's greatness.

Abide with Me

Hebrews 13:1–8

Keep your lives free from the love of money
and be content with what you have, because God has said,
"Never will I leave you; never will I forsake you." *Hebrews 13:5*

One of the highlights of English football (soccer) each year is the final match of the annual FA Cup Final. For more than a hundred years, the day has been marked by excitement, festivity, and competition. But what fascinates me is how the game begins. It starts with the singing of the traditional hymn "Abide with Me."

At first that struck me as odd. What does that hymn have to do with soccer? As I thought about it, though, I realized that for the follower of Christ it has everything to do with sports, shopping, working, going to school, or anything else we do. Since there is no corner of our lives that should not be affected by the presence of God, the longing that He would abide with us is actually the most reasonable thing we could desire. Of course, the presence of our heavenly Father is not something we need to plead for—it is promised to us. In Hebrews 13:5, we read, "God has said, 'Never will I leave you; never will I forsake you.'"

Not only is God's presence the key to our contentment but it is also the promise that can give us wisdom, peace, comfort, and strength—no matter where we are or what we are doing.

♦ ♦ ♦

Our greatest privilege is to enjoy God's presence.

Last Line of Defense

Romans 8:31–39

No, in all these things we are more than conquerors
through him who loved us. *Romans 8:37*

Gettysburg, Pennsylvania, was the site of a battle that turned the tide of America's Civil War. One of the focal points of the conflict was a rocky knoll called Little Round Top where Colonel Joshua Lawrence Chamberlain and the men of the 20th Maine Infantry stood their ground. Some historians believe that had the Confederate troops gotten past Chamberlain's men, the Union army would have been surrounded—possibly leading to the loss of the war. The "20th Maine" was the last line of defense.

Followers of Christ are also engaged in a vital war. As we battle "the devil's schemes" (Ephesians 6:11), we are called to wear the armor of God and to stand firm in the conflict (vv. 10–18).

And like the Gettysburg soldiers, we have a "last line of defense." For us, though, this defense is greater than any human force. In Romans 8:31–39, Paul says that our ultimate confidence is in the undying love of Christ. So complete is our protection that nothing can "separate us from the love of God that is in Christ Jesus our Lord" (v. 39).

When the enemy seems overwhelming and all seems lost, remember, we have an unbeatable last line of defense: "We are more than conquerors through him who loved us" (v. 37).

◆　◆　◆

God's plan always leads to victory.

Helped by Fear

Proverbs 9:1–12

The fear of the LORD is the beginning of wisdom,
and the knowledge of the Holy One is understanding. *Proverbs 9:10*

Fear means different things to different people. To professional golfer Padraig Harrington, it is a motivator to help him perform his very best. In 2008, when he won both the British Open and the PGA Championship, Harrington said, "Yes, fear is a big part of me. I'd like to say that I have all the trust and patience and I'm relaxed. No, that's not my makeup. [Fear] pushes me on. Keeps me getting to the gym. I have to work with it and use it."

Maybe it's the fear of failure, or the fear of losing his edge, but Harrington finds fear to be a useful thing in his professional life.

The follower of Christ can also be helped by fear. We are challenged in the Scriptures to a reverential fear of God, which is the best type of fear there is. It causes us to be concerned about disobeying Him or living in opposition to His ways. It's being in awe of our great God, bowing to His perfect will, and seeking His wisdom for living. To that end, the proverb declares, "The fear of the LORD is the beginning of wisdom, and the knowledge of the Holy One is understanding" (Proverbs 9:10).

◆　◆　◆

By fearing God rightly, we can live wisely in an uncertain world.

Ordinary versus Extraordinary

Hebrews 4:14–16

*In him and through faith in him we may approach God
with freedom and confidence.* Ephesians 3:12

For more than a century, the pinnacle of golf has been to score 59—a score that had been recorded only three times in PGA Tour history before 2010. By the 2019 season, it had been done nine times—and in 2016 Jim Furyk shot an unprecedented 58. Consequently, some sportswriters speculated that the most coveted achievement in golf was now becoming commonplace! That is simply not true. It would be a mistake to begin to view such a low score as ordinary.

For those who follow Jesus Christ, it is also a mistake to view the remarkable as ordinary. Think about prayer, for instance. At any moment we can talk to the Creator God, who spoke the universe into existence! Not only are we welcomed into His presence but we are also invited to enter boldly: "Let us then approach God's throne of grace with confidence, so that we may receive mercy and find grace to help us in time of need" (Hebrews 4:16).

There is nothing ordinary about access to God—yet sometimes we take this privilege for granted. He is almighty God, but He is also our Father who loves us and allows us to call on Him at any moment of any day. Now, that's extraordinary!

◆ ◆ ◆

God is always available to hear the prayers of His children.

Erev Yom Kippur

Matthew 5:21–26

First go and be reconciled to [your brother or sister];
then come and offer your gift. *Matthew 5:24*

In Judaism, the holiest day of the year is Yom Kippur, the Day of Atonement. On that day, the nation seeks God's forgiveness for sins both personal and national.

What is interesting, however, is the day before Yom Kippur, known as Erev Yom Kippur. It represents a person's last opportunity to seek forgiveness from other people before Yom Kippur begins. This is important because, in Jewish thought, you must seek forgiveness from other people before you can seek the forgiveness of God.

Today, we are called to do the same. Jesus pointed out that in order to worship Him with all our heart, we first need to resolve matters with others. In Matthew 5:23–24, He said, "If you are offering your gift at the altar and there remember that your brother or sister has something against you, leave your gift there in front of the altar. First go and be reconciled to [your brother and sister]; then come and offer your gift."

Even in a matter so basic as our giving, the ability to truly worship God is hindered by the reality of relationships broken by our wrong actions, attitudes, and words.

So that our worship can be pleasing and acceptable to God, let us make every effort to be reconciled to one another—today.

◆ ◆ ◆

An offense against your neighbor
is a fence between you and God.

Ebenezer

Psalm 42:1–5

Samuel took a stone. . . . He named it Ebenezer, saying,
"Thus far the LORD has helped us." *1 Samuel 7:12*

In Charles Dickens's *A Christmas Carol,* the central character is Ebenezer Scrooge. As a boy, I enjoyed watching the old black-and-white version of that movie with Alastair Sim portraying Scrooge. Sim did a phenomenal job presenting the heartless, miserly, self-centered Scrooge. I still look in the television schedule each Christmas to learn when I can watch that particular rendition of Dickens's tale.

Years of watching the travails of Scrooge have spoiled something for me though—the name "Ebenezer." I have associated it with Scrooge, but its original meaning was light-years away from that. In 1 Samuel, following a decisive battle with the Philistines, the Israelites erected a stone as a reminder of the Lord's help in the battle. They named that stone *Ebenezer,* which means "Stone of Help," to remind people of how God rescued them from their enemies (7:12).

What a contrast! A name that I had come to associate with man's selfishness can actually serve as a reminder of the readily available help of God. As we move through life, may we focus on the faithfulness of the Lord and not the selfishness of man. Let's look to Him as our true Ebenezer—our help in the challenges of life.

◆　◆　◆

Our only hope here below is help from God above.

Remembrance Day

Luke 22:14–20

He took bread, gave thanks and broke it,
and gave it to them, saying, "This is my body given for you;
do this in remembrance of me." *Luke 22:19*

I was in London's Heathrow Airport waiting for a connecting flight to the US. An announcement came over the public address system stating that it was "Remembrance Day" in the United Kingdom, the day on which people honored those who had died for their country in times of war. The announcement further said that at 11:00 a.m. there would be two minutes of silence and that it would be appreciated if everyone kept that in mind. Thousands of people from all over the world stood in silence as a tribute to the fallen soldiers, sailors, marines, and airmen of the UK.

The desire to remember those who gave their lives for their country is noble. Yet, as meaningful as that is, it cannot compare to the privilege that belongs to us when we approach the Lord's Table. As we celebrate Communion, we are obeying Christ's command that we remember His death (Luke 22:19) and to do it "until he comes" (1 Corinthians 11:26). When He sacrificed His life for us, He provided the forgiveness of sins that sets us free and secures for us an eternal home in heaven.

Rather than letting the Lord's Supper become routine, make every opportunity at the Table a true "Remembrance Day" by honoring Him till He comes.

◆　◆　◆

Remembering Christ's death for us
should cause us to live for Him.

Mighty Waters

Revelation 1:9–17

His feet were like bronze glowing in a furnace,
and his voice was like the sound of rushing waters. *Revelation 1:15*

While in Brazil, I went to see Iguazu Falls, one of the greatest waterfalls in the world. The massive falls are breathtaking, but what impressed me most at Iguazu was not the sight of the falls or the spray of the water. It was the sound. The sound was beyond deafening—I felt as if I was actually inside the sound itself. It was an overwhelming experience that reminded me how small I am by comparison.

Later, with this scene in mind, I couldn't help but think about John in Revelation 1:15. While on the island of Patmos, he saw a vision of the risen Christ. The apostle described Jesus in the glory of His resurrection, noting both His clothing and His physical qualities. Then John described Christ's voice "like the sound of rushing waters" (v. 15).

I'm not sure I fully appreciated what that meant until I visited Iguazu and was overwhelmed by the thundering sound of the falls. As those mighty waters reminded me of my own smallness, I better understood why John fell at the feet of Christ as if dead (v. 17).

Perhaps that description will help you grasp the awesomeness of Jesus's presence and prompt you to follow John's example of worshiping the Savior.

◆　◆　◆

True worship of Christ changes admiration into adoration.

Fast Feet

Philippians 4:10–19

The Sovereign LORD is my strength; he makes my feet like the feet
of a deer, he enables me to tread on the heights. *Habakkuk 3:19*

While in Chile for a Bible conference, I was resting at the hotel when
a rugby match came on television. Though I don't fully understand
rugby, I enjoy it and admire the courage it takes to play such a dangerous sport.

During the match, one of the French players was injured and had
to be taken to the sidelines. As the trainers attended to him, the camera showed a closeup of his shoes. With a black marker the player had
written the words: "Habakkuk 3:19" and "Jesus is the way." Those
expressions of faith and hope were a strong testimony of that young
athlete's priorities and values.

The verse cited on that rugby player's shoes is not just one of
heavenly hope and persevering faith. It is one of practical value—
especially to an athlete dependent on speed for success. It says, "The
Sovereign LORD is my strength; he makes my feet like the feet of a
deer, he enables me to tread on the heights."

In all of life, we need the strength and supply of our God. He
alone can give us "feet" that are swift and strong. He alone can equip
us for all of the uncertainties of life, for He alone is our strength.
With Paul, we can be assured: "My God will meet all your needs"
(Philippians 4:19).

◆　◆　◆

We always have enough when God is our supply.

It's Elementary

Daniel 2:20-22

Known to God from eternity are all His works. *Acts 15:18 (NKJV)*

On a recent trip to London, we exited the Baker Street underground station where we were greeted by a life-size statue of legendary detective Sherlock Holmes. Created by novelist Sir Arthur Conan Doyle, Holmes was an investigative genius who could routinely assess seemingly random clues and solve a mystery.

Baffled by Holmes' uncanny brilliance, his sidekick, Dr. Watson, would ask for an explanation—to which Holmes would glibly respond, "Elementary!" and then proceed to unfold the solution.

If only life operated that way. So often, we face events and circumstances that are far more baffling than a Sherlock Holmes mystery. We struggle to figure life out, but we seem to come up short.

In times like these, it's comforting to know that we have a God who doesn't need to assess the situation—He already knows everything perfectly well. In Acts 15:18 we read, "Known to God from eternity are all His works" (NKJV). He never has to wonder or resort to inductive reasoning.

Despite our finiteness, our lives rest in the hands of the One who knows all the whats, whys, and whens we'll ever face. As we trust in Him, He'll guide us in the path He desires us to take—and His way is never wrong.

◆　◆　◆

In a world of mystery, it's a comfort to know the God
who knows all things.

Patience Needed

1 Corinthians 13

Love is patient, love is kind. It does not envy,
it does not boast, it is not proud. 1 Corinthians 13:4

Our flight to Singapore was delayed because of mechanical problems. The fifteen-minute delay turned into thirty minutes, then sixty—and then three hours. The ground staff was scrambling to calm the crowd, but people were tired and soon became angry. As the night stretched on, the crowd began to turn into a mob—screaming at the staff with harsh language. The pilot even came to offer encouragement, but the crowd turned on him as well.

As I watched the scene unfold, a Singaporean man standing beside me softly said, "Patience will be a much-needed virtue tonight."

Life can be frustrating, even exasperating. Yet, many times impatience is just a reflection of our own self-centeredness in response to life's disappointments. Real love is pictured in the Bible as self-sacrifice (John 15:13), and one demonstration of that love is patience toward others. "Love is patient, love is kind. It does not envy, it does not boast, it is not proud. . . . it is not self-seeking, it is not easily angered" (1 Corinthians 13:4–5). It sets aside our personal agenda and seeks to model Christ.

Sound impossible? It is, if we attempt it in our own strength. But as we pray for help, the Holy Spirit provides us with patience that reflects God's love—even during frustrating circumstances.

◆ ◆ ◆

When tempted to lose patience with others,
remember God's patience with you.

The New Religion

Ecclesiastes 2:1–11

Be on your guard against all kinds of greed;
life does not consist in an abundance of possessions. *Luke 12:15*

Driving through Ireland to a Bible conference, I saw a fascinating billboard. It was large and white with nothing on it but a woman's red shoe and the bold caption: "Is Shopping the New Religion?"

The pursuit of possessions continues to be one of the most powerful motivations that people can experience. But can the accumulation of things bring true satisfaction?

In Luke 12:15, Jesus answered that question with a firm and uncompromising "No!" During a discussion on material wealth, He said, "Be on our guard against all kinds of greed; life does not consist in an abundance of possessions." Life must always be more than just the inventory of the things we own.

King Solomon also attempted to find satisfaction in the pursuit of things. He discovered it to be full of emptiness (Ecclesiastes 2:1–17). If we have placed the "abundance of possessions" we possess at the center of our lives, shopping may, in fact, have become a substitute for God—a new religion. But such endeavors will always result in emptiness.

David prayed, "You open your hand and satisfy the desires of every living thing" (Psalm 145:16). Only God is able to bring real satisfaction to our lives.

◆ ◆ ◆

You are rich when you are satisfied with what you have.

Word Hunger

Psalm 119:97–104

Like newborn babies, crave pure spiritual milk,
so that by it you may grow up in your salvation. *1 Peter 2:2*

I had just completed a night of Bible conference ministry in Kuala Lumpur, Malaysia, and was chatting with some of the people who had attended. At the end of the line was a young man in his twenties. He shared with me that he had been a Christ-follower for only about four months, and he was eager to learn more of the teachings of the Bible. I referred him to the Our Daily Bread Ministries website with the Discovery Series topics as one possible resource for his personal study.

The next night the young man returned to the conference and shared that he had stayed up until 3:30 reading and processing the biblical truths he discovered in that online resource. With a big smile on his face, he declared that he just couldn't get enough of God's Word (1 Peter 2:2).

What spiritual hunger! That excited young man is a reminder to us of the wonder of the Bible and its heart-enriching truths. It's all too easy for us to ignore God's Book in a world filled with voices screaming for our attention. But only in the Bible can we find God's wisdom for our struggles, God's answers for our questions, and God's truths for our understanding. These truths are worth hungering for.

◆　◆　◆

Study the Bible to be wise; believe it to be safe;
practice it to be holy.

Treasure in Heaven

Matthew 6:19–21

Where your treasure is, there your heart will be also. Matthew 6:21

On a teaching trip to Togo, West Africa, I noticed hundreds of abandoned buildings that were only partially built. I asked my missionary host why so many structures were incomplete. His response was striking.

Apparently, Togolese law allows an injured party to demand payment from the available cash of family members of the person who injured them. Even distant relatives are not exempt. To prevent their cash savings from being attached to a legal action, people will purchase land instead. Slowly, sometimes over decades, they will build a house on it with any extra cash. The hundreds of unfinished buildings were testimony to how easy it is to lose one's material possessions.

This was certainly part of the reason our Lord taught, "Do not store up for yourselves treasures on earth, where moths and vermin destroy, and where thieves break in and steal" (Matthew 6:19). Treasures of this world are vulnerable to being lost, stolen, destroyed, or devalued. If that is our focus, we will only experience frustration.

If our hearts are drawn instead to the value of the eternal—godly character, relationships, souls—we won't be disappointed. We will become rich in the things of Christ. And treasure in heaven can never be taken away!

◆　◆　◆

Those who live for God can expect trouble in the world.

Heart of Gratitude

Psalm 19:1–6

The heavens declare the glory of God;
the skies proclaim the work of his hands. *Psalm 19:1*

My boyhood hero was American frontiersman Davy Crockett. In the book *David Crockett: His Life and Adventures*, Davy encounters a beautiful sight that causes him to launch into praise to the Creator. The writer describes it this way: "Just beyond the grove there was another expanse of treeless prairie, so rich, so beautiful, so brilliant with flowers, that even Colonel Crockett, all unaccustomed as he was to the devotional mood, reined in his horse, and gazing entranced upon the landscape, exclaimed, 'O God, what a world of beauty hast Thou made for man! And yet how poorly does he requite Thee for it! He does not even repay Thee with gratitude.'" Crockett recognized that the Creator's handiwork demands a response of thankfulness—a response that is often neglected or ignored.

The psalmist wrote, "The heavens declare the glory of God; the skies proclaim the work of his hands" (Psalm 19:1). God's handiwork is a spectacle that, rightly understood, should not only take our breath away but should also inspire us to worship and praise our God as it did the psalmist.

Davy Crockett was right—encountering the wonders of God's creation should inspire, at the least, a heart of gratitude. Are we grateful?

◆ ◆ ◆

God's glory shines through His creation.

Serious Business

Psalm 96:1–13

"The LORD reigns."
The world is firmly established, it cannot be moved;
he will judge the peoples with equity. *Psalm 96:10*

Recently I was called for jury duty. It meant extraordinary inconvenience and lots of lost time, but it was also serious business. During the first day's orientation, the judge lectured us on the responsibility at hand and the important nature of the task. We were going to sit in judgment of people who either had disputes (civil court) or were charged with crimes (criminal court). I felt a great sense of inadequacy for the task at hand. Passing judgment on another person, with serious life consequences riding on the decision, is not a simple thing. Because we're flawed human beings, we may not always make the right judgments.

While the justice systems of our world might struggle and falter because of the inherent failings of the humans who manage them, we can always trust our God to excel in wisdom and fairness. The psalmist sang, "'The LORD reigns.' The world is firmly established, it cannot be moved; he will judge the peoples with equity." (Psalm 96:10). God judges according to righteousness—defined by His own perfect justice and flawless character.

We can trust God now when life seems unfair, knowing that He will one day make all things right in His final court (2 Corinthians 5:10).

◆　◆　◆

One day God will right every wrong.

Joyful Reunion

2 Timothy 4:1–8

> He who testifies to these things says, "Yes, I am coming soon."
> Amen. Come, Lord Jesus. *Revelation 22:20*

Some years ago when our children were still young, I flew home after a ten-day ministry trip. In those days people were allowed to visit the airport boarding area to greet incoming passengers. When my flight landed, I came out of the jet-bridge and was greeted by our little ones—so happy to see me that they were screaming and crying. I looked at my wife, whose eyes were teary. I couldn't speak. Strangers in the gate area also teared up as our children hugged my legs and cried their greetings. It was a wonderful moment.

The memory of the intensity of that greeting serves as a gentle rebuke to the priorities of my own heart. The apostle John, eagerly desiring Jesus's return, wrote, "He who testifies to these things says, 'Yes, I am coming soon.' Amen. Come, Lord Jesus." (Revelation 22:20). In another passage, Paul even spoke of a crown awaiting those who have "have longed for [Jesus's] appearing" (2 Timothy 4:8). Yet sometimes I don't feel as eager for Christ's return as my children were for mine.

Jesus is worthy of the very best of our love and devotion—and nothing on earth should compare to the thought of seeing Him face-to-face. May our love for our Savior deepen as we anticipate our joyful reunion with Him.

◆ ◆ ◆

Those who belong to Christ should be longing to see Him.

Greater Compassion

Isaiah 49:13–18

Can a mother forget the baby at her breast
and have no compassion on the child she has borne?
Though she may forget,
I will not forget you! *Isaiah 49:15*

I first met my wife, Marlene, in college. I was majoring in pastoral studies, and she was working on a degree in elementary education. The first time I saw her working with children, I knew what a natural fit this was for her. She loved children. It became even more obvious when we got married and had children of our own. Seeing her with them was an education in unconditional love and acceptance. It was clear to me that there is nothing in all the world like the tender love and compassion of a mother for her newborn child.

That's what makes Isaiah 49:15 so remarkable. It's here that God told His people, who were feeling forsaken and forgotten (v. 14), that His compassion is even greater than a mother's: "Can a mother forget the baby at her breast and have no compassion on the child she has borne? Though she may forget, I will not forget you!"

Sometimes we face struggles in life, and we are tempted to think that God has forgotten us. We may even believe that God no longer loves us. But God's love for us is as expansive as the open arms of Christ on the cross. And the tender compassion of our heavenly Father is more dependable and more enduring than the love of a nursing mother for her infant. Be comforted—His love never fails.

◆　◆　◆

God's love for us is as expansive
as the open arms of Christ on the cross.

"I Know Everything"

Psalm 139:1–12

You discern my going out and my lying down;
you are familiar with all my ways. *Psalm 139:3*

Our son and daughter-in-law had an emergency. Our grandson Cameron was suffering from pneumonia and bronchitis and needed to go to the hospital. They asked if we could pick up their five-year-old son, Nathan, from school and take him home. Marlene and I were glad to do so.

When Nathan got in the car, Marlene asked, "Are you surprised that we came to get you today?" He responded, "No!" When we asked why not, he replied, "Because I know everything!"

A five-year-old can claim to know everything, but those of us who are a bit older know better. We often have more questions than answers. We wonder about the whys, whens, and hows of life—often forgetting that though we do not know everything, we know the God who does.

Psalm 139:1 and 3 speak of our all-knowing God's intimate all-encompassing, understanding of us. David says, "You have searched me, LORD, and you know me. . . . You discern my going out and my lying down; you are familiar with all my ways." How comforting to know God loves us perfectly, is fully aware of what we will face today, and He knows how best to help us in every circumstance of life.

Our knowledge will always be limited, but knowing God is what matters most. We can trust Him.

◆ ◆ ◆

Knowing God is what matters most.

Your Journey

John 14:15–21

"I will not leave you as orphans; I will come to you." John 14:18

I grew up in the rebellious 1960s and turned my back on religion. I had attended church all my life but didn't come to faith until my early twenties after a terrible accident. Since that time, I have spent my adult years telling others of Jesus's love for us. It has been a journey.

Certainly "a journey" describes life in this broken world. On the way we encounter mountains and valleys, rivers and plains, crowded highways and lonely roads—highs and lows, joys and sorrows, conflict and loss, heartache and solitude. We can't see the road ahead, so we must take it as it comes, not as we wish it would be.

The follower of Christ, however, never faces this journey alone. The Scriptures remind us of the constant presence of God. There is nowhere we can go that He is not there (Psalm 139:7–12). He will never leave us or forsake us (Deuteronomy 31:6; Hebrews 13:5). Jesus, after promising to send the Holy Spirit, told His disciples, "I will not leave you as orphans; I will come to you" (John 14:18).

The challenges and opportunities we face on our journey can be met confidently, for God has promised us His never-failing presence.

◆ ◆ ◆

**Faith never knows where it is being led,
but it loves and knows the One who is leading.** —*Oswald Chambers*

Jehovah-Jireh

Matthew 6:5–15

Your Father knows what you need before you ask him. Matthew 6:8

In my early years as a pastor, I served in small churches where finances were often tight. Sometimes our family finances felt the weight of that pressure. On one occasion, we were down to the last of our food, and payday was still several days away. While my wife and I fretted about how we would feed our kids in the next few days, our doorbell rang. When we opened the door, we discovered two bags of groceries. We had not told anyone of our plight, yet our provider God had led someone to meet that need.

This reminds me of the Old Testament account of Abraham when he was asked to sacrifice his son Isaac. At just the right moment, God provided a ram instead. Abraham called this place Jehovah-Jireh, "The Lord Will Provide" (Genesis 22:14). He is the One who still cares deeply for His children.

Jesus said, "Your Father knows what you need before you ask him" (Matthew 6:8). He is constantly caring for and seeking the best for us—a reminder that in times of hardship, need, and fear, we have Someone who cares. Peter wrote that we can cast all our cares upon Jesus, because He cares for us (1 Peter 5:7). We can turn to Him in our time of need.

◆ ◆ ◆

God provides the power we need to persevere.

Be Still

Philippians 4:4–9

And the peace of God, which transcends all understanding,
will guard your hearts and your minds in Christ Jesus. *Philippians 4:7*

As I sat in the dentist's chair, I braced myself for the drilling that would begin my root canal. I was ready for the worst, and my body language and facial expression exposed my sense of dread. The dentist looked at me and smiled, saying, "It's okay, Bill. Try to relax."

That isn't easy to do. It is actually very difficult to try (requiring effort and exertion) to relax (requiring an absence of effort and exertion). "Try" and "relax" just don't seem to fit together—not only in the dentist's chair but in the spiritual realm as well.

Far too often I don't limit my efforts of resistance to visits at the dentist's office. In my relationship with Christ, I find myself not pressing for God's purposes but for my own interests. In those moments, the hardest thing for me to do is "try to relax" and genuinely trust God for the outcome of life's trials.

In Psalm 46:10, we read, "Be still, and know that I am God; I will be exalted among the nations, I will be exalted in the earth." In the moments when my heart is anxious, this verse reminds me to "be still, and know." Now, if I can only put that into practice and rest confidently in His care, I'll be at peace.

◆　◆　◆

God knows the future, so we are safe in His hands.

Untended Places

Psalm 119:9–16

I have hidden your word in my heart,
that I might not sin against you. *Psalm 119:11*

Our family had just arrived at the lake cottage we had rented for a week of much-anticipated vacation when my wife discovered the unmistakable evidence of spiders and mice in the house. It wasn't that we had never encountered such things, but that we had expected the cottage to be cleaned and prepared for our stay there. Instead, the counters, cabinets, and beds were littered with the residue of infestation, requiring much cleaning before we settled in. It wasn't a bad house; it had just been left untended.

We might be guilty of dealing with our hearts the way that cottage was managed. Our "untended places" can become breeding grounds for infestations of wrong thinking, poor attitudes, or sinful behavior—creating problems that require significant attention to correct. The wise path is to recognize our need to tend our hearts by staying in God's Word and embracing its truths.

In Psalm 119:11, the psalmist recognized the danger of not building our lives on the Scriptures. He said, "I have hidden your word in my heart, that I might not sin against you."

With a focus on the Word, we can build strong spiritual lives that will help us avoid the dangers that inevitably grow in untended places.

◆ ◆ ◆

To grow spiritually strong, read the Word.

Granville Sharp

James 1:19–27

Do not merely listen to the word, and so deceive yourselves.
Do what it says. *James 1:22*

When I was a Bible college student, a name occasionally mentioned in Greek class was that of Granville Sharp. He was a renowned Greek scholar (1735–1813) whose studies resulted in principles of biblical interpretation that continue to guide our understanding of the original language of the New Testament.

To study the Scriptures and learn the powerful truths they contain is a noble exercise, but no matter how deeply we study, it is not enough. James challenged us to understand this when he wrote: "Do not merely listen to the word, and so deceive yourselves. Do what it says. Anyone who listens to the word but does not do what it says is like someone who looks at his face in a mirror and, after looking at himself, goes away and immediately forgets what he looks like." (James 1:22–24).

Granville Sharp understood this and put his faith into practice. In addition to being a biblical scholar, he also fought to eradicate slavery in England. Sharp said, "A toleration of slavery is, in effect, a toleration of inhumanity." His biblical understanding of the worth of a human soul and the justice of a holy God compelled him to act on his beliefs.

We can benefit from Sharp's passion for the Word—and for living out the truth that Word contains.

◆　◆　◆

We don't really know the Bible unless we obey the Bible.

What Matters Most

1 John 4:7–19

*He sent his one and only Son into the world
that we might live through him.* 1 John 4:9

As Jesus's beloved disciple John grew older, his teaching became increasingly narrowed, focusing entirely on the love of God in his three letters. In the book *Knowing the Truth of God's Love*, Peter Kreeft cites an old legend, which says that one of John's young disciples once came to him complaining, "Why don't you talk about anything else?" John replied, "Because there isn't anything else."

God's love is certainly at the heart of the mission and message of Jesus. In his earlier gospel account, John recorded the words, "For God so loved the world that he gave his one and only Son, that whoever believes in him shall not perish but have eternal life" (John 3:16).

The apostle Paul tells us that God's love is at the core of how we live, and he reminds us that "neither death nor life, neither angels nor demons, neither the present nor the future, nor any powers, neither height nor depth, nor anything else in all creation, will be able to separate us from the love of God that is in Christ Jesus our Lord" (Romans 8:38–39).

God's love is so strong, available, and stabilizing that we can confidently step into each day knowing that the good things are gifts from His hand and the challenges can be faced in His strength. For all of life, His love is what matters most.

◆　◆　◆

God's love stands when all else has fallen.

The Need
for Nourishment

Psalm 37:1–11

Trust in the LORD and do good;
dwell in the land and enjoy safe pasture. *Psalm 37:3*

Our grandson Cameron was born six weeks prematurely. Undersized and in danger, he became a resident of the hospital's neonatal unit for about two weeks until he gained enough weight to go home. His biggest challenge was that, in the physical exercise of eating, he burned more calories than he was taking in. This obviously hindered his development. It seemed that the little guy took two steps backward for every step of progress he made.

No medicine or treatment could solve the problem; he just needed the strength-giving fortification of nourishment.

As followers of Christ, we are constantly finding our emotional and spiritual reserves drained by the challenges of life in a fallen world. In such times, we need nourishment to strengthen us. In Psalm 37, David encouraged us to strengthen our hearts by feeding our souls. He wrote, "Trust in the LORD and do good; dwell in the land and enjoy safe pasture" (v. 3).

When weakness inevitably afflicts us, the reassurance of God's never-ending faithfulness can enable us to carry on in His name. His faithful care is the nourishment we need, giving us, as the hymn "Great Is Thy Faithfulness" says, "strength for today, and bright hope for tomorrow."

◆ ◆ ◆

Feed on God's faithfulness to find the strength you need.

Invisible Man

John 14:5–20

Fixing our eyes on Jesus, the pioneer and perfecter of faith.
For the joy set before him, he endured the cross. Hebrews 12:2

As a boy, I was fascinated by the book *The Invisible Man* by H. G. Wells. The main character played an elaborate game of hide-and-seek, staying just out of reach of mere mortals "cursed" with a visible nature. To have a physical presence, he wore clothes and wrapped his face in bandages. When it was time to escape, he simply removed everything and disappeared.

I wonder if we have similar thoughts about our unseen God. We feel He is beyond our reach and express it in song with one of my favorite hymns: "Immortal, invisible, God only wise, / In light inaccessible hid from our eyes."

Yet, while declaring the wonder of God, the hymn speaks of a God who is not just invisible: "All praise we would render—O help us to see / 'Tis only the splendor of light hideth Thee!"

We perceive that God is distant, far off, inaccessible, and hidden. But we need a God who is accessible, and we wonder how to have a meaningful relationship with Him.

We will never fully comprehend what God is like. Yet He himself is accessible to us. In part, that is why Jesus came—to "show us the Father" (John 14:8) and to bring us close to Him, because "The Son is the image of the invisible God" (Colossians 1:15).

Our God is an invisible God, beyond our limited comprehension. Thankfully, Jesus came to show us how near to us He really is.

◆ ◆ ◆

God's presence with us is His greatest present to us.

Making a Masterpiece

2 Corinthians 5:12–21

*If anyone is in Christ, the new creation has come: The old has gone,
the new is here!* 2 Corinthians 5:17

One of my earliest memories of my dad is that he loved doing paint-by-number pictures. The canvas was large, but the numbered segments where a predetermined color would go were very small. Dad would sit in his chair in our basement for hours, working meticulously with his painting in front of him and a cup of coffee at his side.

As a boy, I would sit on the basement stairs and watch with fascination. My interest did not stem from a misguided thought that doing paint-by-number work made my dad a great artist. Rather, I was amazed at how patiently he would work on each painting. Finally, the thousands of slivers of color became an image that Dad considered well worth the effort.

As I think of my dad's patience in bringing a painting to life, my heart is directed to our heavenly Father. He looks on us and sees the voids and imperfections in our lives, yet He lovingly and patiently does His work in us to make us His masterpiece—a masterpiece that "conform[s] to the image of his Son" (Romans 8:29).

What a joy it is to have such a God, who makes us new (2 Corinthians 5:17) and never tires of investing His energy and effort into our lives!

◆　◆　◆

Only God can transform a sin-stained soul
into a masterpiece of grace.

Flexibility

James 4:13–17

Instead, you ought to say, "If it is the Lord's will,
we will live and do this or that." *James 4:15*

Over the years, it has been my privilege to lead several study trips to the Bible lands. In the months leading up to our group's departure, we would have a series of orientation meetings in preparation for our trip. Schedules, hotel accommodations, contact information—all of which could be changed at a moment's notice.

For that reason, our preparation times always stressed the need for flexibility. A willingness to go with the flow and adjust to whatever changes we might encounter was especially valuable. Life has an element of unpredictability for which flexibility is the best response.

James expressed a worldview of flexibility in chapter four of his letter. While it is wise to plan for the future, we must do so with the recognition that God's purposes might be different from ours. Instead of rigidly saying, "Today or tomorrow we will go to this or that city" (v. 13), James counseled us to flex to God's direction in our lives. He said, "Instead, you ought to say, 'If it is the Lord's will, we will live and do this or that'" (v. 15).

The adventure of following Christ is one that rests in His perfect plans—and flexibility helps us to be prepared for wherever His purposes might take us.

◆　◆　◆

A man's heart plans his way,
but the Lord directs his steps. —*Proverbs 16:9*

Hope Is For . . .

Hebrews 10:19–25

Let us hold unswervingly to the hope we profess,
for he who promised is faithful. *Hebrews 10:23*

Although I try not to be shocked by the things I see these days, I was caught off-balance by the message on the woman's T-shirt as she walked past me in the mall. The bold letters declared: "Hope Is for Suckers." Certainly, being naïve or gullible can be foolish and dangerous. Disappointment and heartache can be the tragic offspring of unfounded optimism. But not allowing oneself to have hope is a sad and cynical way to view life.

Biblical hope is unique; it's a confident trust in God and what He is doing in the world and in our lives. That's something everyone needs! The writer to the Hebrews clearly stated the importance of hope when he wrote, "Let us hold unswervingly to the hope we profess, for he who promised is faithful" (Hebrews 10:23).

Having biblical hope is not foolish, because it has a strong foundation. We hold fast to the hope we have received in Christ because our God is faithful. He can be trusted with anything and everything we will ever face—both for today and forever. Our hope is grounded in the trustworthy character of the God who loves us with an everlasting love. So, the T-shirt had it wrong. Hope is not for suckers; it's for you and for me!

◆　◆　◆

Hope that has its foundation in God
will not crumble under the pressures of life.

Wonderfully Made

Psalm 139:13–18

Your works are wonderful,
I know that full well. *Psalm 139:14*

While I was getting an eye exam recently, my doctor hauled out a piece of equipment that I hadn't seen before. I asked him what the device was, and he responded, "I'm using it to take a picture of the inside of the back of your eye."

I was impressed that someone had invented a camera that could do that. But I was even more impressed by what my doctor could learn from that picture. He said, "We can gather a lot of details about your current general health simply by looking at the back of your eye."

It is remarkable that a person's overall health can be measured by the health of the eye. What care the Lord has taken to place these details in the bodies He created! It immediately brings to my mind the words of David, the psalmist, who reveled in God's creativity: "I praise you because I am fearfully and wonderfully made; your works are wonderful, I know that full well" (Psalm 139:14).

The enormous complexities of our bodies reflect the genius and wisdom of our great Creator. The wonder of His design is more than breathtaking—it gives us countless reasons to worship Him!

◆　◆　◆

All life is created by God and bears His autograph.

Momma's Rules

Ephesians 4:17–32

*You were taught, with regard to your former way of life,
to put off your old self, which is being corrupted
by its deceitful desires.* Ephesians 4:22

I met a delightful woman named "Momma Charlie," who has raised a dozen or so foster kids. These youngsters were assigned to her by the courts, and she gave them a home with stability, guidance, and love. She told me that every time a new child arrived, the first order of business was to explain "Momma's Rules." These included behavioral standards, plus chores that would provide much-needed help in the busy household while teaching accountability to kids with little previous training.

Some of the children may have balked at "Momma's Rules," thinking they were robbing them of fun or pleasure—yet nothing would be further from the truth. Those standards allowed for an orderly household where both Momma and the children could find life enjoyable and peaceful.

Similarly, some look at the standards God set forth in the Bible as obstacles that prevent us from enjoying life. However, the boundaries God places actually protect us from our worst inclinations and foster healthy responses to Him.

In Ephesians 4, for example, Paul provides some guidance for how we are to live. As we live by these and other loving instructions from God, we find protection and the opportunity for true, lasting joy.

◆ ◆ ◆

God's Word is the compass that keeps us on course.

True Sacrifice

Romans 5:6–11

Greater love has no one than this:
to lay down one's life for one's friends. *John 15:13*

Eric was one of the good guys. As a police officer, he saw his work as service to his community, and he was fully committed to serving at all costs. Evidence of this desire was seen on the door of Eric's locker at the police station, where he posted John 15:13.

In that verse, our Lord said, "Greater love has no one than this: to lay down one's life for one's friends." Those words, however, were not merely noble ideals. They expressed Eric's commitment to his duty as a police officer—a commitment that demanded the ultimate price when he was killed in the line of duty. It was a real-life display of the heart of true sacrifice.

Jesus Christ lived out the powerful words of John 15:13 within hours of stating them. The upper room event where Jesus spoke of such sacrifice was followed by communion with the Father at Gethsemane, a series of illegal trials, and then crucifixion before a mocking crowd.

As the Son of God, Jesus could have avoided the suffering, torture, and cruelty. He was utterly without sin and did not deserve to die. But love, the fuel that drives true sacrifice, drove Him to the cross. As a result, we can be forgiven if we will accept His sacrifice and resurrection by faith. Have you trusted the One who laid down His life for you?

◆ ◆ ◆

Only Jesus, the perfect sacrifice, can declare guilty people perfect.

I'm Bored

John 10:7–14

I have come that they may have life,
and have it to the full. *John 10:10*

When our kids were teens, we repeatedly had the following discussion after their church youth group meeting: I asked, "How was youth group tonight?" And they responded, "It was boring." After several weeks of this, I decided to find out for myself. I slipped into the gym where their meeting was held, and I watched. I saw them participating, laughing, listening—having a great time. That night on the way home I asked about their evening and, once again, they said, "It was boring." I responded, "I was there. I watched. You had a great time!" They responded, "Maybe it wasn't as bad as usual."

I recognized that behind their reluctance to admit they were enjoying youth group were things such as peer pressure and a fear of not appearing "cool." But then I wondered, Am I similarly afraid to get too excited about spiritual things?

Indeed, there is nothing in this universe more worthy of our enthusiasm than who Christ is and what He did for us. Jesus said, "I have come that they may have life, and have it to the full" (John 10:10). That's the opposite of boring! At any age, we have a gift from the Savior that is worth celebrating. Our salvation is something to get excited about!

◆　◆　◆

If you know Christ, you always have a reason to celebrate.

Leading from the Front

Psalm 23

> He leads me beside quiet waters,
> he refreshes my soul.
> He guides me along the right paths
> for his name's sake. *Psalm 23:2–3*

Stephen Ambrose's book *Band of Brothers* follows the US Army's Easy Company from training in Georgia through the Normandy Invasion on D-Day (June 6, 1944) and ultimately to the end of World War II in Europe. For the bulk of that time, Easy Company was led by Richard Winters. Winters was an especially good officer because he led from the front. The most commonly heard words from Winters in combat were, "Follow me!" Other officers may have sought the safety of the rear areas, but if Winters' men were going into combat, he was going to lead them.

Jesus is the one true Leader of His children. He knows what we need and where we are most vulnerable. His leading is part of what makes Psalm 23 the most beloved song in the Bible's hymnal. In verse 2, David says that the Shepherd "leads me beside quiet waters," and in verse 3 he adds, "He guides me along the right paths for his name's sake." These twin ideas reveal why His care is so complete. Whether it is times of refreshing and strengthening ("quiet waters") or seasons of doing what pleases Him ("right paths"), we can follow Him.

Our Lord knows the way. Let's follow Him.

◆ ◆ ◆

Jesus knows the way—all we need to know is how to follow Him!

No Risk

Ephesians 2:1–10

*For it is by grace you have been saved, through faith—
and this is not from yourselves, it is the gift of God.* Ephesians 2:8

A colleague recently shared an experience I don't intend to try personally—bungee jumping. I found his description of the event both fascinating and terrifying. To think of jumping headfirst from a bridge hundreds of feet in the air suspended only by a giant rubber band is not my idea of a good time. But his leap was not without support. He described not one, but two heavy-duty harnesses that secured him to his lifeline—and to safety. The careful design and proven testing of those harnesses gave him great confidence as he jumped into the air.

As I listened, it occurred to me that for the follower of Christ, living in a sinful world is not a blind "leap of faith." We too have a pair of protections that can secure us in even the darkest times of life. In Ephesians 2:8–9, Paul wrote these words, "For it is by grace you have been saved, through faith—and this is not from yourselves, it is the gift of God—not by works, so that no one can boast."

It's in these twin harnesses—God's grace and faith in the finished work of Jesus—that our relationship with God safely rests. In the strength of these provisions, salvation is not a risky leap into the void. It's an exercise of confidence in God's Word and His unfailing love and protection.

♦ ♦ ♦

We can expect God's peace when we accept God's grace.

Battling Ego

James 4:6–10

God resists the proud, but gives grace to the humble. James 4:6 (NKJV)

When a general returned from a victorious battle, ancient Rome would stage a parade to welcome the conqueror home. The parade would include the general's troops, as well as trophy captives who had been brought along as evidence of the victory. As the parade made its way through the city, the crowds would cheer their hero's success.

To prevent the general's ego from becoming unduly swollen, a slave rode along with him in his chariot. Why? So that as the Roman throngs heaped praise on the general, the slave could continually whisper in his ear, "You too are mortal."

When successful, we too may lose sight of our own frailty and allow our hearts to fill with destructive pride. James pointed us away from the danger of pride by pointing us to humility and to God. He wrote, "God resists the proud, but gives grace to the humble" (James 4:6 NKJV). The key to that statement is *grace*. Nothing is more wonderful! The Lord alone deserves thanks and praise—especially for the grace He has lavished on us.

Our achievements, success, or greatness are not rooted in ourselves. They are the product of God's matchless grace, upon which we are eternally dependent.

◆　◆　◆

God's grace is infinite love expressing itself
through infinite goodness.

Too Blessed

Psalm 107:1–8

Let them give thanks to the LORD for his unfailing love
and his wonderful deeds for mankind. *Psalm 107:8*

On my daily commute to and from the office, I have plenty of time for reading—bumper stickers on cars, that is. Some are surly, others are clever, and still others are downright distasteful. One bumper sticker I saw recently, however, gently challenged my heart about the way I often engage life. The sticker simply said, "Too blessed to complain."

I must confess that I felt convicted as I pondered those words. Too often I find myself lamenting moments in life that don't go my way, rather than focusing on the wonderful gifts my heavenly Father has given me. Reading that simple message that day brought me a renewed commitment to be more actively and intentionally grateful, because my God has been good to me in more ways than I could ever count.

Psalm 107 is a song that seeks to rectify thankless thinking. The psalmist (who many think was King David) makes a plea to hearts grown cold with ingratitude, repeating four times, "Let them give thanks to the LORD for his unfailing love and his wonderful deeds for mankind" (vv. 8, 15, 21, 31). Even in the worst of times, we have much to be thankful for. May we learn to thank God for His goodness to us!

◆　◆　◆

We don't need more to be thankful for,
we just need to be more thankful.

The Other Eighty Percent

Psalm 69:29–36

Let heaven and earth praise him,
the seas and all that move in them. Psalm 69:34

Recently I saw a billboard stating that eighty percent of all life on Earth is found in the seas. That staggering number is difficult to process, largely because most of that life is out of sight.

As I considered this, it reminded me of how much greater God's creation is than we typically appreciate. While we can easily have our breath taken away by a majestic mountain range or a panoramic sunset, we sometimes fail to see His extraordinary work in the details that require more careful study and examination. Not only is much of God's creation hidden by the oceans but other parts are also too small for our eyes to observe. From the microscopically small to the unsearched reaches of the universe, it is all the work of our Creator. In those magnificent structures—seen and unseen—God's creative glory is revealed (Romans 1:20).

As we grow to understand the wonder of creation, it must always point us to the Creator himself—and it calls us to worship Him. As the psalmist said, "Let heaven and earth praise him, the seas and all that move in them" (Psalm 69:34). If creation itself gives praise to the Creator, we should certainly join the chorus. What a mighty God we serve!

◆ ◆ ◆

The wonder of creation causes us to say, "What a wonderful God!"

The Joy
of Disappointment

Proverbs 3:1–12

Trust in the LORD with all your heart
and lean not on your own understanding. *Proverbs 3:5*

While in Bible college, I auditioned for one of the school's traveling musical teams. I was excited about the thought of being able to be involved in that ministry, but I was crushed when I failed to make the team. In my disappointment, I could only trust that God's purposes were greater than mine.

Months later, I had the opportunity to join a different musical team—this time as the Bible teacher. The results were more than I could have imagined. Not only was my future wife a part of that team, allowing us to serve Christ together, but it also gave me many opportunities to preach over the next three years—priceless preparation for a life of ministry in the Word.

Many times we struggle with the reality that our Father knows what is best. We assume our way is right. But as we rest in Him, His purposes always prove to be for our good and His praise. To be honest, that's easy to see when the outcome is better than we had hoped, but it is difficult when we can't see the good right now—or until we reach heaven.

As wise King Solomon said, "Trust in the LORD with all your heart and lean not on your own understanding; in all your ways submit to him, and he will make your paths straight" (Proverbs 3:5–6).

◆ ◆ ◆

God's purpose for today's events may not be seen until tomorrow.

Almost Content?

1 Timothy 6:6–12

Be content with what you have, because God has said,
"Never will I leave you; never will I forsake you." *Hebrews 13:5*

As I stepped into the restaurant parking lot after lunch, I saw a pickup truck speeding through the parked vehicles. While observing the driver's reckless behavior, I noticed the words on the truck's front license plate. It read, "Almost Content." After thinking about that message and the sentiment it tried to communicate, I concluded that the concept "almost content" doesn't exist. Either we are content or we are not.

Admittedly, contentment is a tough needle to thread. We live in a world that feeds our desire for more and more—until we find it almost impossible to be content with anything. But this is nothing new. The book of Hebrews addressed this issue, saying, "Keep your lives free from the love of money and be content with what you have, because God has said, 'Never will I leave you; never will I forsake you'" (13:5). The only remedy for hearts that "want it all" is the contentment found in the presence of the living God. He is sufficient for our needs and longings, and He alone can bring us the peace and contentment we'll never find in the pursuits of this life.

Almost content? There is no such thing. In Christ we can know true contentment.

◆ ◆ ◆

Contentment is not getting what we want
but being satisfied with what we have.

Coade Stone

1 Peter 2:1–10

Come to him, the living Stone—rejected by humans
but chosen by God and precious to him. *1 Peter 2:4*

Throughout London, there are statues and other items made from a unique building material called Coade stone. Developed by Eleanor Coade for her family business in the late 1700s, this artificial stone is virtually indestructible and has the capacity to withstand time, weather, and man-made pollution. Although it was a marvel during the Industrial Revolution, Coade stone was phased out in the 1840s following Eleanor's death, and it was replaced by Portland cement as a building material. In spite of that, however, there remain today dozens of examples of this sturdy, ceramic-like stone that have withstood the harsh London environment for more than 200 years.

The apostle Peter described Jesus as a living stone. He wrote, "Come to him, the living Stone—rejected by humans but chosen by God and precious to him—you also, like living stones, are being built up into a spiritual house" (1 Peter 2:4–5). Precious in the eyes of the Father is the sacrifice of the Rock of our salvation. Christ is the enduring stone upon which the Father has built our salvation and the only foundation for meaningful life (1 Corinthians 3:11).

It is only as our lives are built upon His strength that we will be able to endure the harshness of life in a fallen world.

◆　◆　◆

We have nothing to fear if we stay close to the Rock of Ages.

Wonderful!

Job 42:1–6

Surely I spoke of things I did not understand,
things too wonderful for me to know. *Job 42:3*

As our plane began its descent, the flight attendant read the long list of arrival information as if she were reading it for the thousandth time that day—no emotion or interest as she droned on about our impending arrival. Then, with the same tired, disinterested voice, she finished by saying, "Have a wonderful day." The dryness of her tone contrasted with her words. She said "wonderful" but in a manner completely absent of any sense of wonder.

Sometimes I fear that we approach our relationship with God in the same way: Routine. Bored. Apathetic. Disinterested. Through Christ, we have the privilege of being adopted into the family of the living God, yet often there seems to be little of the sense of wonder that should accompany that remarkable reality.

Job questioned God about his suffering, but when challenged by Him, Job was humbled by the wonder of his Creator and His creation. Job replied, "You asked, 'Who is this that obscures my plans without knowledge?' Surely I spoke of things I did not understand, things too wonderful for me to know" (Job 42:3).

I long for the wonder of God to take hold of my heart. Accepted by God through faith in Jesus Christ—what a wonderful reality!

◆ ◆ ◆

Nothing can fill our hearts more than the wonder
of our God and His love.

Place of Water

Psalm 63

The water I give them will become in them a spring
of water welling up to eternal life. *John 4:14*

East Africa is one of the driest places on earth, which is what makes *Nairobi* such a significant name for a city in that region. The name comes from a Masai phrase meaning "cold water," and it literally means "the place of water."

Throughout history, the presence of water has been both life-giving and strategic. Whether a person lives in a dry climate or a rainforest, water is a nonnegotiable necessity. In a dry and barren climate, knowing where to find the place of water can mean the difference between life and death.

Our spiritual life also has certain nonnegotiable elements. That is why Jesus, upon encountering a spiritually thirsty woman at a well, declared to her that He alone could provide living water. He told her, "Whoever drinks the water I give them will never thirst. Indeed, the water I give them will become in them a spring of water welling up to eternal life" (John 4:14).

Like the deer that pants for water (mentioned in Psalm 42:1–2), our souls thirst for God and long for Him (63:1). We desperately need the sustenance that comes only from Jesus Christ. He is the source of living water that refreshes our hearts.

◆ ◆ ◆

Jesus is the fountain of living water.

The Wonder of the Cross

Hebrews 12:1–4

Fixing our eyes on Jesus, the pioneer and perfecter of faith.
For the joy set before him he endured the cross. *Hebrews 12:2*

While visiting Australia, I had the opportunity on a particularly clear night to see the Southern Cross. Located in the Southern Hemisphere, this constellation is one of the most distinctive. Mariners and navigators began relying on it as early as the fifteenth century for direction and navigation through the seas. Although relatively small, it is visible throughout most of the year. The Southern Cross was so vivid on that dark night that even I could pick it out of the bundle of stars. It was truly a magnificent sight!

The Scriptures tell us of an even more magnificent cross—the cross of Christ. When we look at the stars, we see the handiwork of the Creator. However, when we look at the cross, we see the Creator dying for His creation. Hebrews 12:2 calls us to fix "our eyes on Jesus, the pioneer and perfecter of faith. For the joy set before him he endured the cross, scorning its shame, and sat down at the right hand of the throne of God."

Here is the wonder of Calvary's cross: While we were still in our sins, our Savior died for us (Romans 5:8). Those who place their trust in Christ are reconciled to God, and He navigates them through life (2 Corinthians 1:8–10).

Christ's sacrifice on the cross is the greatest of all wonders!

◆ ◆ ◆

Christ's cross provides the only safe crossing into eternity.

City of Refuge

Psalm 59:10–17

I will sing of your strength,
in the morning I will sing of your love;
for you are my fortress,
my refuge in times of trouble. *Psalm 59:16*

As we entered a town in Australia, we were greeted by a sign that declared: "We welcome all who are seeking refuge and asylum." This kind of welcome seems to resonate with the Old Testament concept of the cities of refuge. In the Old Testament era, cities of refuge (Numbers 35:6) were established to be a safe haven for people who had accidentally killed someone and were needing protection. God had the people establish such cities to provide that refuge.

This concept, however, was not intended to be simply a practice for ancient Israel. More than that, cities of refuge reflected the heart of God for all people. He himself longs to be our safe haven and our city of refuge in the failures, heartaches, and losses of life. We read in Psalm 59:16–17, "I will sing of your strength, in the morning I will sing of your love; for you are my fortress, my refuge in times of trouble. You are my strength, I sing praise to you; you, God, are my fortress, my God on whom I can rely."

For the hurting heart of every generation, our "city of refuge" is not a place. Our city of refuge is a Person—the God who loves us with an everlasting love. May we find our refuge and rest in Him.

◆　◆　◆

Refuge can be found in the Rock of Ages.

Not Lost in Translation

Romans 8:19–27

The Spirit intercedes for God's people
in accordance with the will of God. *Romans 8:27*

Over the years, I've had the opportunity to teach the Bible to many people around the world. Because I speak only English, I often work with interpreters who can take the words of my heart and translate them into the language of the people. Effective communication is directly dependent upon the skill of these translators. Whether it is Inawaty in Indonesia, Annie in Malaysia, or Jean in Brazil, they ensure that the meaning of my words is clearly expressed.

This work of translation resembles one facet of the work of the Holy Spirit in the life of God's people. In our times of prayer, we don't always know how we should pray (Romans 8:26), and verse 27 encourages us, saying, "He who searches our hearts knows the mind of the Spirit, because the Spirit intercedes for God's people in accordance with the will of God." When we go to our heavenly Father in prayer, the Holy Spirit comes to our aid by translating our prayers according to God's good purposes for our lives.

What a provision! Not only does God desire for us to share our hearts with Him but He also provides us with the greatest interpreter to help us as we pray. We can be sure that our prayers will never get lost in translation.

◆ ◆ ◆

The participation of the Spirit assures
that my prayers line up with God's purposes.

Mistaken Identity

Matthew 16:13–20

> "But what about you?" [Jesus] asked.
> "Who do you say I am?" *Matthew 16:15*

My youngest brother, Scott, was born when I was a senior in high school. This age difference made for an interesting situation when he grew to college age. On his first trip to his college campus, I went along with him and our mom. When we arrived, people thought we were Scott Crowder and his dad and his grandmom. Eventually, we gave up correcting them. No matter what we said or did, our actual relationships were overridden by this humorous case of mistaken identity.

Jesus questioned the Pharisees about His identity: "What do you think about the Messiah? Whose son is he?" "The son of David," they replied (Matthew 22:42). The identity of Messiah was critical, and their answer was correct but incomplete. The Scriptures had affirmed that Messiah would come and reign on the throne of His father David. But Jesus reminded them that though David would be Christ's ancestor, the Christ would also be more—David referred to Him as "Lord."

Faced with a similar question, Peter rightly answered, "You are the Messiah, the Son of the living God" (Matthew 16:16). Still today, the question of Jesus's identity rises above the rest in significance—and it is eternally important that we make no mistake in understanding who He is.

◆　◆　◆

No mistake is more dangerous
than mistaking the identity of Jesus.

Tears of Gratitude

1 Corinthians 11:23–32

You proclaim the Lord's death until he comes. *1 Corinthians 11:26*

At a communion service my wife and I attended, the congregation was invited to come forward to receive the bread and cup from one of the pastors or elders. They told each one personally of Jesus's sacrifice for him or her. It was an especially moving experience during what can often become just routine. After we returned to our seats, I watched as others slowly and quietly filed past. It was striking to see how many had tears in their eyes. For me, and for others I talked with later, they were tears of gratitude.

The reason for tears of gratitude is seen in the reason for the communion table itself. Paul, after instructing the church at Corinth about the meaning of the memorial supper, punctuated his comments with these powerful words: "For whenever you eat this bread and drink this cup, you proclaim the Lord's death until he comes" (1 Corinthians 11:26). With the elements of communion pointing directly to the cross and the sacrifice of Christ on our behalf, that service was about so much more than ritual—it was about Christ. His love. His sacrifice. His cross. For us.

How inadequate are our words to convey the extraordinary worth of Christ! Sometimes tears of gratitude speak what words can't fully express.

◆　◆　◆

**The love Christ showed for us on the cross
is greater than words could ever express.**

An Appropriate Name

Matthew 1:18–25

You are to give him the name Jesus. *Matthew 1:21*

The name of the southeastern Asian nation of Indonesia is formed by combining two Greek words that together mean "island." That name is appropriate because Indonesia is made up of more than 17,500 islands spanning nearly 750,000 square miles. Indonesia—an appropriate name for a nation of islands.

In the Bible, we find that people were often given names—sometimes at birth, sometimes later—that made a statement about them or their character. Barnabas, whose name means "son of encouragement," continually encouraged those he encountered. Jacob, whose name means "schemer," repeatedly manipulated people and situations for his own selfish ends.

And no one has ever been more appropriately named than Jesus. When the angel of the Lord spoke to Joseph about Mary's soon-to-be-born Son, he told Joseph, "You are to give him the name Jesus, because he will save his people from their sins" (Matthew 1:21).

Jesus means "the Lord saves" and defines both who Jesus is and why He came. He was also called Immanuel, which means "God with us" (1:23). His name reveals our eternal hope!

◆ ◆ ◆

The name of Jesus is at the heart of our faith and our hope.

Kangaroos and Emus

Philippians 3:12–17

Forgetting what is behind . . . I press on toward the goal
to win the prize for which God has called me
heavenward in Christ Jesus. *Philippians 3:13–14*

Two of Australia's indigenous creatures, kangaroos and emus, have something in common—they seldom move backward. Kangaroos, because of the shape of their body and the length of their strong tail, can bounce along with forward movement, but they cannot shift easily into reverse. Emus can run fast on their strong legs, but the joints in their knees seem to make backward movement difficult. Both animals appear on Australia's coat of arms as a symbol that the nation is to be ever moving forward and making progress.

The apostle Paul called for a similar approach to the life of faith in his letter to the Philippians: "Brothers and sisters, I do not consider myself yet to have taken hold of it. But one thing I do: Forgetting what is behind and straining toward what is ahead, I press on toward the goal to win the prize for which God has called me heavenward in Christ Jesus" (3:13–14).

While it is wise to learn from the past, we shouldn't live in the past. We cannot redo or undo the past, but by God's grace we can press forward and serve God faithfully today and in the future. The life of faith is a journey forward as we become like Christ.

◆ ◆ ◆

I will go anywhere—provided it is forward.

Crowns of Honor

John 19:1–8

The soldiers twisted together a crown of thorns and put it on his head. John 19:2

The Crown Jewels of the United Kingdom are stored securely and protected within the Tower of London under twenty-four-hour guard. Each year, millions visit the display area to "ooh and aah" over these ornate treasures. The Crown Jewels symbolize the power of the kingdom, as well as the prestige and position of those who use them.

Part of the Crown Jewels are the crowns themselves. There are three different types: the coronation crown, which is worn when an individual is crowned monarch; the state crown (or coronet), which is worn for various functions; and the consort crown worn by the wife of a reigning king. Different crowns serve different purposes.

The King of heaven, who was worthy of the greatest crown and the highest honor, wore a very different crown. In the hours of humiliation and suffering that Christ experienced before He was crucified, "the soldiers twisted together a crown of thorns and put it on his head. They clothed him in a purple robe" (John 19:2). That day, the crown, which is normally a symbol of royalty and honor, was turned into a tool of mockery and hate. Yet our Savior willingly wore that crown for us, bearing our sin and shame.

The One who deserved the best of all crowns took the worst for us.

◆ ◆ ◆

Without the cross, there could be no crown.

Look to the Hills

Psalm 121

I lift up my eyes to the mountains—
where does my help come from?
My help comes from the LORD,
the Maker of heaven and earth. *Psalm 121:1–2*

Atop Corcovado Mountain overlooking the city of Rio de Janeiro, Brazil, stands Christ the Redeemer, one of the tallest statues of Christ in the world. Standing thirty meters tall, with arms spreading twenty-eight meters, this sculpture weighs 700 tons. It can be seen day or night from almost anywhere in the city. One look to the hills brings this figure of Christ the Redeemer into view.

The New Testament tells us that Christ is not only the Redeemer but He is also the Creator of the universe, and that Creator is in view in Psalm 121. There the psalmist challenges us to lift our eyes to the hills to see God, for our "help comes from the LORD, the Maker of heaven and earth" (vv. 1–2). He alone is sufficient to be our strength and to guide our steps as we make our way through a dangerous and troubled world.

We lift our eyes to the One who keeps us (v. 3), guards us (vv. 5–6), and overshadows us in the face of all types of danger. He preserves us from evil and keeps us safely in His care for all eternity (vv. 7–8).

In faith, we lift our eyes to the One who is our Redeemer and Creator. He is our help and our hope and our eternal home.

◆ ◆ ◆

Christ was lifted up that He might lift us up.

Big Spring

John 4:7–14

The water I give them will become in them a spring of water welling up to eternal life. John 4:14

In Michigan's Upper Peninsula is a remarkable natural wonder—a pool about forty feet deep and three feet across, which Native Americans called "Kitch-iti-kipi," or "the big cold water." Today it is known as The Big Spring. It is fed by underground springs that push more than 10,000 gallons of water a minute through the rocks below and up to the surface. Additionally, the water keeps a constant temperature of forty-five degrees Fahrenheit, meaning that even in the brutally cold winters of the Upper Peninsula the pool never freezes. Tourists can enjoy viewing the waters of Big Spring during any season of the year.

When Jesus encountered a woman at Jacob's well, He talked to her about another source of water that would always satisfy. But He did not speak of a fountain, spring, river, or lake. He said, "Whoever drinks the water I give them will never thirst. Indeed, the water I give them will become in them a spring of water welling up to eternal life" (John 4:14).

Far greater than any natural spring is the refreshment we have been offered in Christ himself. We can be satisfied, for Jesus alone, the Water of Life, can quench our thirst. Praise God, for Jesus is the source that never runs dry.

❖　❖　❖

The only real thirst-quencher is Jesus—the living water.

With Him Forever!

2 Corinthians 4:16–18

So we fix our eyes not on what is seen,
but on what is unseen, since what is seen is temporary,
but what is unseen is eternal. *2 Corinthians 4:18*

In 1859, during the turbulent years prior to America's Civil War, Abraham Lincoln had the opportunity to speak to the Agricultural Society in Milwaukee, Wisconsin. As he spoke, he shared with them the story of an ancient monarch's search for a sentence that was "true and appropriate in all times and situations." His wise men, faced with this heady challenge, gave him the sentence, "And this too shall pass away."

This is certainly true of our present world—it is constantly in the process of deterioration. And it's not happening just to the world; we also face the reality in our own lives that our days are numbered. James wrote, "What is your life? You are a mist that appears for a little while and then vanishes" (James 4:14).

Although our current life is temporary and will pass away, the God we worship and serve is eternal. He has shared that eternity with us through the gift of His Son, Jesus Christ. He promises us a life that will never pass away: "For God so loved the world that he gave his one and only Son, that whoever believes in him shall not perish but have eternal life" (John 3:16).

When Christ returns, He will take us home to be with Him forever!

◆　◆　◆

For hope today, remember the end of the story—
eternity with God.

Disposable Culture

Psalm 136:1–9, 23–26

Give thanks to the LORD, for he is good.
His love endures forever. Psalm 136:1

More than ever, we live in a disposable culture. Think for a minute about some of the things that are made to be thrown away—razors, water bottles, lighters, paper plates, plastic eating utensils. Products are used, tossed, and then replaced.

This disposable culture is also reflected in more significant ways. Many times true commitment in relationships is seen as optional. Marriages struggle to survive. Long-term employees are discharged just before retirement for cheaper options. A highly revered athlete leaves to join another team. It seems as if nothing lasts.

Our unchanging God, however, has promised that His loving mercy endures forever. In Psalm 136, the singer celebrates this wonderful promise by making statements about God's wonder, work, and character. He then punctuates each statement about God with the phrase, "His love endures forever." Whether it is the wonder of His creation (vv. 4–9), the rescue of His people (vv. 10–22), or His tender care for His own (vv. 23–26), we can trust Him because His love will never fail. In a temporary world, the permanence of God's mercy gives us hope. We can sing with the psalmist, "Give thanks to the LORD, for he is good! His love endures forever" (v. 1).

◆ ◆ ◆

God's grace is immeasurable; His mercy inexhaustible;
His peace inexpressible.

What Love Is

1 John 3:16–18

*Dear children, let us not love with words or speech
but with actions and in truth.* 1 John 3:18

Years ago I asked a young man who was engaged to be married, "How do you know that you love her?" It was a loaded question, intended to help him look at his heart's motives for the upcoming marriage. After several thoughtful moments, he responded, "I know I love her because I want to spend the rest of my life making her happy."

We discussed what that meant—and the price tag attached to the selflessness of constantly seeking the best for the other person, rather than putting ourselves first. Real love has a lot to do with sacrifice.

That idea is in line with the wisdom of the Bible. In the Scriptures there are several Greek words for *love*, but the highest form is *agape* love—love that is defined and driven by self-sacrifice. Nowhere is this more true than in the love our heavenly Father has shown us in Christ. We are deeply valued by Him. Paul stated, "God demonstrates his own love for us in this: While we were still sinners, Christ died for us" (Romans 5:8).

If sacrifice is the true measure of love, there could be no more precious gift than Jesus: "For God so loved the world that he gave his one and only Son" (John 3:16).

◆　◆　◆

The measure of love is what you are willing to give up for it.

Perception or Reality?

Mark 4:35–51

Teacher, don't you care if we drown? *Mark 4:38*

We often hear it said, "Perception is reality." That idea for Americans may have dawned on September 26, 1960—the date of the first televised debate between two presidential candidates. In front of the cameras, John Kennedy appeared composed; Richard Nixon appeared nervous. The perception was that Kennedy would be a stronger leader. The debate not only turned that election but it also changed the way politics is done in the US. Politics by perception became the rule of the day.

Sometimes perception is reality. But not always—especially our perceptions about God. When Jesus and His disciples were crossing the Sea of Galilee in a small fishing vessel, a sudden storm threatened to sink the boat. With Jesus asleep and the disciples on the verge of panic, they began to stir Him, asking, "Teacher, don't you care if we drown?" (Mark 4:38).

Their question sounds similar to questions I've asked. At times I perceive God's apparent inactivity as a lack of care. But His care for me goes well beyond what I can see or measure. Our God is deeply concerned for what concerns us. He urges us to place all our care upon Him, "for He cares for [us]" (1 Peter 5:7 NKJV). That is true reality.

◆ ◆ ◆

Even when we don't sense God's presence,
His loving care is all around us.

The Wonder of Sight

Genesis 1

> I will praise you because I am fearfully and wonderfully made;
> your works are wonderful,
> I know that full well. *Psalm 139:14*

On the livescience.com website, I read something pretty amazing: "If you were standing atop a mountain surveying a larger-than-usual patch of the planet, you could perceive bright lights hundreds of miles distant. On a dark night, you could even see a candle flame flickering up to thirty miles away." No telescopes or night-vision goggles needed—the human eye is so profoundly designed that even long distances can be spanned with clear sight.

This fact is a vivid reminder of our amazing Creator, who designed not only the human eye but also all of the details that make up our expansive universe. And, unlike anything else in creation, God has made us in His own image (Genesis 1:26). "In the image of God" speaks of something far greater than the ability to see. It speaks of a likeness to God that makes it possible for us to be in relationship with Him.

We can affirm David's declaration, "I will praise you because I am fearfully and wonderfully made; your works are wonderful, I know that full well" (Psalm 139:14). Not only have we been given eyes to see but we have also been made so that, in Christ, one day we will see Him!

◆　◆　◆

All of God's creation bears witness to Him as our great Creator.

Longing for Rescue

Luke 1:26–38

You will conceive and give birth to a son,
and you are to call him Jesus. He will be great
and will be called the Son of the Most High. *Luke 1:31–32*

When the movie *Man of Steel* was released in 2013, it was a fresh imagining of the Superman story. Filled with breathtaking special effects and nonstop action, it drew crowds to movie theaters around the world. Some said the film's appeal was rooted in its amazing technology. Others pointed to the enduring appeal of the "Superman mythology."

Amy Adams, the actress who played Lois Lane in the movie, has a different view of Superman's appeal. She says it is about a basic human longing: "Who doesn't want to believe that there's one person who could come and save us from ourselves?"

That's a great question. And the answer is that someone has already come to save us from ourselves, and that someone is Jesus. Several announcements were made regarding the birth of Jesus. One of them was from the angel Gabriel to Joseph: "[Mary] will give birth to a son, and you are to give him the name Jesus, because he will save his people from their sins" (Matthew 1:21).

Jesus came—He did so to save us from our sin and from ourselves. His name means "the Lord saves"—and our salvation was His mission. The longing for rescue that fills the human heart ultimately is met by Jesus.

◆　◆　◆

Jesus's name and mission are the same—He came to save us.

Foley Artists

John 16:7–15

Satan himself masquerades as an angel of light. 2 Corinthians 11:14

Crunch. Crunch. Whoosh! In the early days of film, Foley artists created sounds to support the story's action. Squeezing a leather pouch filled with cornstarch made the sound of snow crunching, shaking a pair of gloves sounded like bird wings flapping, and waving a thin stick made a whoosh sound. To make movies as realistic as possible, these artists used creative techniques to replicate sounds.

Like sounds, messages can be replicated. One of Satan's most frequently used techniques is that of replicating messages in spiritually dangerous ways. Paul warns in 2 Corinthians 11:13–14, "For such people are false apostles, deceitful workers, masquerading as apostles of Christ. And no wonder, for Satan himself masquerades as an angel of light." Paul is warning us about false teachers who turn our attention away from Jesus Christ and the message of His grace.

Jesus said that one purpose of the Holy Spirit living in us is that "when he, the Spirit of truth, comes, he will guide you into all the truth" (John 16:13). With the help and guidance of the Spirit, we can find the safety of truth in a world of counterfeit messages.

♦ ♦ ♦

The Holy Spirit is our ever-present Teacher.

Firm Foundation

Matthew 7:21–27

Everyone who hears these words of mine and puts them into practice is like a wise man who built his house on the rock. *Matthew 7:24*

Earthquakes are prevalent in the Pacific Rim region known as the "Ring of Fire." Ninety percent of the world's earthquakes and eighty-one percent of the world's largest earthquakes occur there. I learned that many buildings in the city of Hong Kong have been built on granite, which could help minimize damage in the event of an earthquake. The foundation of buildings is especially important in earthquake-prone regions of the world.

Jesus Christ told His followers that a stable foundation is critical in building lives. He said, "Everyone who hears these words of mine and puts them into practice is like a wise man who built his house on the rock. The rain came down, the streams rose, and the winds blew and beat against that house; yet it did not fall, because it had its foundation on the rock" (Matthew 7:24–25). The foundation of Jesus Christ is what will give us the stability our hearts and lives need now and into the future.

By allowing the Lord's wisdom to guide us in our relationships, decisions, and priorities, we find that He provides the most trustworthy foundation any life could be built upon.

◆　◆　◆

Jesus is the best foundation upon which to build a solid life.

Heart of Joy

John 15:9–17

I have told you this so that my joy may be in you
and that your joy may be complete. *John 15:11*

While waiting in the gate area of Singapore's Changi Airport to board my flight, I noticed a young family—mom, dad, and son. The area was crowded, and they were looking for a place to sit. Suddenly, the little boy began loudly singing "Joy to the World." He was about six years old, so I was pretty impressed that he knew all the words.

What captured my attention even more was the look on the boy's face—his beaming smile matched the words he was singing as he proclaimed to everyone at the gate the joy of the Christ who has come.

This joy is not limited to exuberant children nor should it be confined to the Christmas season. The overflowing joy of knowing Christ's presence in our lives was one of the themes of Jesus's final teaching with His disciples the night before He died on the cross. He told them of His extravagant love for them—that He loved them as the Father loved Him (John 15:9). After sharing what this eternal relationship looks like, Jesus said, "I have told you this so that my joy may be in you and that your joy may be complete" (v. 11).

What a promise! Through Jesus Christ our hearts can be filled with joy—real joy!

◆　◆　◆

In every season of life, we can know joy in Christ.

Motivated by Love

2 Corinthians 5:11–17

Christ's love compels us. *2 Corinthians 5:14*

In the 1920s, Bobby Jones dominated the golfing world, despite being an amateur. In one film about his life, *Bobby Jones: Stroke of Genius*, there is a scene where a professional golfer asks Bobby when he is going to quit being an amateur and grab for the money like everyone else does. Jones answers by explaining that the word *amateur* comes from the Latin *amo*—"to love." His answer was clear: He played golf because he loved the game.

Our motives, why we do what we do, make all the difference. This certainly applies to those who are followers of Jesus Christ. In his letter to the Corinthian church, Paul gives us an example of this. Throughout the epistle he defended his conduct, character, and calling as an apostle of Christ. In response to those who questioned his motives for ministry, Paul said, "Christ's love compels us, because we are convinced that one died for all, and therefore all died. And he died for all, that those who live should no longer live for themselves but for him who died for them and was raised again" (2 Corinthians 5:14–15).

Christ's love is the greatest of all motivators. It causes those who follow Him to live for Him, not for themselves.

◆　◆　◆

We are shaped and fashioned by what we love most.

Light in the Darkness

John 12:42–50

I have come into the world as a light, so that no one who believes in me should stay in darkness. John 12:46

During a trip to Peru, I visited one of the many caves found throughout that mountainous country. Our guide told us that this particular cave had already been explored to a depth of nine miles—and it went even deeper. We saw fascinating bats, nocturnal birds, and interesting rock formations. Before long, however, the darkness of the cave became unnerving—almost suffocating. I was greatly relieved when we returned to the surface and the light of day.

That experience was a stark reminder of how oppressive darkness can be and how much we need light. We live in a world made dark by sin—a world that has turned against its Creator. And we need the Light.

Jesus, who came to restore all of creation—including humanity—to its intended place referred to himself as that "light" (John 8:12). "I have come into the world as a light," He said, "so that no one who believes in me should stay in darkness" (12:46).

In Him, we not only have the light of salvation but also the only light by which we can find our way—His way—through our world's spiritual darkness.

◆　◆　◆

When we walk in the Light, we won't stumble in the darkness.

A Loving Father

Psalm 103:7–13

As a father has compassion on his children,
so the LORD has compassion on those who fear him. *Psalm 103:13*

The parents were obviously weary from dragging their two energetic preschoolers through airports and airplanes, and now their final flight was delayed. As I watched the two boys running around the crowded gate area, I wondered how Mom and Dad were going to keep the little guys settled down for our half-hour flight into Grand Rapids. When we finally boarded, I noticed that the father and one of the sons were in the seats behind me. Then I heard the weary father say to his son, "Why don't you let me read one of your storybooks to you." And during the entire flight, this loving father softly and patiently read to his son, keeping him calm and focused.

In one of his psalms David declares, "As a father has compassion on his children, so the LORD has compassion on those who fear him" (Psalm 103:13). The tender word *compassion* gives us a picture of how deeply our heavenly Father loves His children, and it reminds us what a great gift it is to be able to look to God and cry, "Abba, Father" (Romans 8:15).

God longs for you to listen again to the story of His love for you when you are restless on your own journey through life. Your heavenly Father is always near, ready to encourage you with His Word.

◆　◆　◆

God's great love for His child is one of His greatest gifts.

Darkness and Light

Psalm 91:1–8

You will not fear the terror of night, . . .
nor the pestilence that stalks in the darkness. *Psalm 91:5–6*

When I was a boy, I delivered newspapers to about 140 homes on two streets that were connected by a cemetery. Since I delivered a morning newspaper, I had to be out at 3:00 a.m. walking through that cemetery in the darkness. Sometimes I would be so frightened that I would actually run! I was afraid until I was standing safely under a streetlight on the other side. The scary darkness was dispelled by the light.

The psalmist understood the connection between fear and darkness, but he also knew that God is greater than those fears. He wrote, "You will not fear the terror of night, nor the arrow that flies by day, nor the pestilence that stalks in the darkness" (Psalm 91:5–6). Neither terrors of night nor evil in the darkness need to drive us to fear. We have a God who sent His Son, the Light of the World (John 8:12).

In the light of God's love and grace and truth, we can find courage, help, and strength to live for Him.

◆ ◆ ◆

You need not fear the darkness
if you are walking with the Light of the World.

Unpredictable

Psalm 46

Be still, and know that I am God;
I will be exalted among the nations,
I will be exalted in the earth. *Psalm 46:10*

At the 2003 US Women's Open, the relatively unknown Hilary Lunke secured the greatest prize in women's golf—and a place in history. Not only did she win the US Open in an 18-hole playoff but it was also her only professional victory. Her surprising and inspiring win underscores the fact that one of the most exciting things about sports is its unpredictability.

The unpredictability of life is not always so thrilling, however. We devise and strategize. We make plans, projections, and proposals about what we would like to see happen in life, but often they are little more than our best guess. We have no idea what a year, a month, a week, or even a day might bring. So we pray and plan, and then we trust the God who knows fully and completely what we can never predict. That is why I love the promise of Psalm 46:10: "Be still, and know that I am God; I will be exalted among the nations, I will be exalted in the earth."

Life is unpredictable. There are countless things I can never know with certainty. What I can know, however, is that there is a God who knows all and loves me deeply. And by knowing Him, I can "be still"—I can be at peace.

◆　◆　◆

God's care is the certainty we take into life's uncertainties.

The Waving Girl

Romans 15:1–7

Accept one another, then, just as Christ accepted you,
in order to bring praise to God. Romans 15:7

In the late 1800s and early 1900s, a familiar sight greeted ships as they pulled into the port of Savannah, Georgia. That sight was Florence Martus, "The Waving Girl." For forty-four years, Florence greeted the great ships from around the world, waving a handkerchief by day or a lantern by night. Today, a statue of Florence and her faithful dog stands in Savannah's Morrell Park, permanently welcoming incoming vessels.

There is something in a warm welcome that speaks of acceptance. In Romans 15:7, Paul urged his readers: "Accept one another, then, just as Christ accepted you." Paul had in view our treatment of each other as followers of Christ, for in verses five and six he challenged us to live in harmony with one another. The key is to have "the same attitude of mind toward each other that Christ Jesus had, so that with one mind and one voice you may glorify the God and Father of our Lord Jesus Christ."

Our acceptance of our fellow believers in Christ demonstrates more than just our love for each other—it reflects the great love of the One who has permanently welcomed us into His family.

◆ ◆ ◆

The closer Christians get to Christ,
the closer they get to one another.

The Cross and the Crown

John 19:21–30

*I am the resurrection and the life. He who believes in Me,
though he may die, he shall live.* John 11:25 (NKJV)

Westminster Abbey in London has a rich historical background. In the tenth century, Benedictine monks began a tradition of daily worship there that still continues today. The Abbey is also the burial place of many famous people, and every English monarch since AD 1066 has been crowned at the Abbey. In fact, seventeen of those monarchs are also buried there—their rule ending where it began.

No matter how grandiose their burial, world rulers rise and fall; they live and die. But another king, Jesus, though once dead, is no longer buried. In His first coming, Jesus was crowned with thorns and crucified as the "king of the Jews" (John 19:3, 19). Because Jesus rose from the dead in victory, we who are believers in Christ have hope beyond the grave and the assurance that we will live with Him forever. Jesus said, "I am the resurrection and the life. He who believes in Me, though he may die, he shall live. And whoever lives and believes in Me shall never die" (11:25–26 NKJV).

We serve a risen King! May we gladly yield to His rule in our lives now as we look forward to the day when the "Lord God Almighty" will reign for all eternity (Revelation 19:6).

◆ ◆ ◆

Jesus's resurrection spelled the death of death.

Also by Bill Crowder

◆　◆　◆

Before Christmas

For This He Came

God of Surprise

Let's Talk

Living with Courage

Moving Beyond Failure

My Hope Is in You

Overcoming Life's Challenges

Seeing the Heart of Christ

The Spotlight of Faith

Trusting God in Hard Times

Windows on Christmas

Windows on Easter

Help us get the word out!

Our Daily Bread Publishing exists to feed the soul with the Word of God.

If you appreciated this book, please let others know.

- Pick up another copy to give as a gift.
- Share a link to the book or mention it on social media.
- Write a review on your blog, on a book-seller's website, or at our own site (odb.org/store).
- Recommend this book for your church, book club, or small group.

Connect with us:

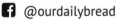 @ourdailybread

 @ourdailybread

 @ourdailybread

Our Daily Bread Publishing
PO Box 3566
Grand Rapids, Michigan 49501 USA

✉ books@odb.org